WARRIOR • 165

US ARMY PARATROOPER IN THE PACIFIC THEATER 1943–45

GORDON L ROTTMAN

ILLUSTRATED BY BRIAN DELF

Series editor Marcus Cowper

First published in Great Britain in 2012 by Osprey Publishing
Midland House, West Way, Botley, Oxford OX2 0PH, UK
44-02 23rd St, Suite 219, Long Island City, NY 11101, USA
E-mail: info@ospreypublishing.com

OSPREY PUBLISHING IS PART OF THE OSPREY GROUP

A CIP catalog record for this book is available from the British Library

Print ISBN: 978 1 78096 129 3
PDF e-book ISBN: 978 1 78096 130 9
EPUB e-book ISBN: 978 1 78096 131 6

Editorial by Ilios Publishing Ltd, Oxford, UK (www.iliospublishing.com)
Page layout by: Mark Holt
Index by Marie-Pierre Evans
Typeset in Sabon and Myriad Pro
Originated by PDQ Media, Bungay, UK
Printed in China through Worldprint Ltd

12 13 14 15 16 10 9 8 7 6 5 4 3 2 1

www.ospreypublishing.com

Back Cover and Title Page photographs: Courtesy of Tom Laemlein, Armor
Plate Press.

ACKNOWLEDGMENTS

The author is indebted to Tom Laemlein of Armor Plate Press for his
invaluable photographic support.

AUTHOR'S NOTE

Osprey Warrior 26: *US Paratrooper 1941–45*, describes the experiences of a
paratrooper in the European Theater during World War II. This book's focus
is on the Southwest Pacific Theater. There will be some duplication of
material in *US Paratrooper 1941–45* and some areas not addressed in this
book that are covered in the former. Other Osprey books on this subject
include: Battle Orders 26: *US Airborne Units in the Pacific Theater 1942–45*;
Elite 31: *US Army Airborne 1940–90*; and Elite 136: *World War II Airborne
Warfare Tactics*.

ARTIST'S NOTE

Readers may care to note that the original paintings from which the
colour plates in this book were prepared are available for private sale.
All reproduction copyright whatsoever is retained by the Publishers.
All enquiries should be addressed to:

Brian Delf,
7 Burcot Park,
Burcot,
Abingdon,
OX14 3DH
United Kingdom

The Publishers regret that they can enter into no correspondence upon
this matter.

THE WOODLAND TRUST

Osprey Publishing is supporting the Woodland Trust, the UK's leading
woodland conservation charity, by funding the dedication of trees. To
celebrate the Queen's Diamond Jubilee we are proud to support the
Woodland Trust's Jubilee Woods Project.

ABBREVIATIONS

Abn Div	Airborne Division
CO	Commanding officer
DZ	Drop zone
HQ	Headquarters
Inf	Infantry
NCO	Noncommissioned officer
OD	Olive drab
PIR	Parachute Infantry Regiment
Prcht	Parachute
PRCT	Parachute Regimental Combat Team
XO	Executive officer (2nd in command)

CONTENTS

US ARMY PARATROOPER, PACIFIC THEATER 1943–45

INTRODUCTION

The environment, enemy and tactical situation experienced by paratroopers in the Pacific were entirely different from those experienced in Europe. Parachute operations were smaller and often conducted on extremely difficult and, in some instances, very dangerous terrain. There was also no significant use of gliders. Furthermore, the Pacific Theater paratroopers conducted amphibious assaults and fought on jungle-covered hills, in swamps and in mud.

There were two US Army airborne units in the Pacific: the 11th Airborne Division (Abn Div) with the 511th Parachute Infantry Regiment (PIR) and the 503rd Parachute Regimental Combat Team (PRCT). While it was proposed that the 503rd PRCT should be assigned to the 11th Abn Div, MacArthur wisely kept the units separate, keeping the 503rd for rapidly emerging special purpose missions. As well as the 511th PIR, the 11th Abn Div ("Angels") included two glider infantry regiments – the 187th and 188th. In July 1945 the 188th became a PIR and the newly arrived to the Philippines 541st PIR was broken up and absorbed into the 11th.

The 503rd PRCT was an independent unit with organic artillery and engineers. It was originally the 503rd PIR, which was organized from two existing parachute infantry battalions at Ft Benning, Georgia, in early 1942. The unit benefited from eight months of collective training prior to deployment to Australia. It was only in theater for a month before its first combat operation.

The 503rd PRCT was initially based in Australia and later on Mindoro Island in the Philippines. It conducted three parachute assaults. The first, at Nadzab on New Guinea, was the first successful US regimental parachute assault anywhere and the only jump in which an entire regiment was delivered at once in the Pacific. The next was Noemfoor Island in the Netherlands East Indies. This was a reinforcement jump in support of an amphibious landing followed by a lengthy jungle mop-up. The last jump, which took place on Corregidor, was considered to be the most dangerous parachute assault of the war in any theater. The regiment went on to land by sealift on Negros Island in the Philippines and endured a grueling fight to clear the mountainous island. With the war's end, the regiment was broken up and inactivated. The short-service men were reassigned to the 11th Abn Div and the long-service men returned home for discharge.

The 511th PIR was raised at Camp Toccoa, GA. After infantry training it went to Ft Benning and went through parachute training. It then undertook

A jumper comes in easy on Corregidor. Many did not experience as good a landing as this man. While camouflage pattern canopies were the norm, many of the parachutes used on Corregidor were white training canopies. (Tom Laemlein, Armor Plate Press)

seven months of training at Camp Mackall, GA and Camp Polk, Louisiana, before deploying to New Guinea where it trained for another five months. The 511th saw its first combat from November 18, 1944, on Leyte, where it landed from ships unopposed and went on to fight a grueling battle in the rain-soaked mountains. There, it conducted only small-scale, piecemeal parachute operations to drop personnel into the near inaccessible combat zone. On Luzon it conducted a parachute assault supporting the rest of the division as it landed amphibiously. The 511th then fought a vicious battle into Manila during February 4–22, 1945. Later, its 1st Bn conducted a daring parachute/amphibious raid to liberate civilian internees at Los Baños[1] and a parachute-delivered attempt to cut off retreating Japanese forces on North Luzon. After the Japanese surrender the division was flown into Japan for occupation duty.

1 See Osprey Raid 14, *The Los Baños Prison Camp Raid*.

CHRONOLOGY

1940

July 1   Parachute Test Platoon formed at Ft Benning, GA.

September 16 1st Prcht Bn activated at Ft Benning and redesignated
                  501st Prcht Bn on October 1.

1941

August 22   503rd Prcht Inf Bn activated at Ft Benning.

October 5   504th Prcht Inf Bn activated at Ft Benning.

December 7   Japanese attack on Pearl Harbor.

1942

March 2   503rd PIR activated at Ft Benning with 503rd and 504th Prcht
                  Inf Bns becoming 1st and 2nd Bns.

March 21   Airborne Command activated at Ft Benning with administrative
                  and training control over airborne units. Command moved to
                  Ft Bragg, NC on April 9.

May 6   Parachute School and 1st Prcht Training Regt activated at
                  Ft Benning.

June 8   3/503rd PIR activated at Ft Benning.

July   2/503rd PIR depart for Scotland.

October   503rd PIR (-) depart California and 501st Prcht Inf Bn depart
                  Panama for Australia.

November 2   2/503rd PIR redesignated 2/509th PIR in Scotland and 501st Prcht
                  Inf Bn redesignated new 2/503rd PIR upon arrival in Australia.

1943

January 5   511th PIR activated at Camp Toccoa, GA.

February 23   11th Abn Div activated at Camp Mackall.
                  511th PIR moved to Camp Mackall, NC and assigned to
                  11th Abn Div on February 25.

May 14   511th PIR moved to Ft Benning for jump training.

June 14   511th PIR return to Camp Mackall.

August 18–20 503rd PIR flown from Australia to New Guinea.

September 5   503rd PIR conduct para assault on Nadzab, New Guinea.

December 6–11 511th PIR take part in the Knollwood Maneuvers.

1944

January 5	511th PIR moved to Camp Polk, LA.
January 17	503rd PIR flown to Australia.
March 1	Airborne Command redesignated Airborne Center and relocated to Camp Mackall.
April 14	503rd PIR flown to New Guinea.
April	511th PIR moved to Camp Stoneman, CA.
May	511th PIR shipped from California to New Guinea.
July 3–4	503rd PIR (-) conduct para assault on Noemfoor Island.
November 9	503rd PIR shipped to Leyte.
November 18	511th PIR shipped to Leyte.
December 15	503rd PIR conduct amphibious assault on Mindoro.

1945

January 15	503rd PIR (-) conduct para assault on Corregidor.
February 3	511th PIR (-) conduct para assault on Tagaytay Ridge, Luzon.
February 4–22	511th PIR engage in the battle for Manila.
February 23	1/511th PIR liberate Los Baños internee camp, Luzon.
February–April	511th conduct operations on southern Luzon.
April 7	503rd PIR commenced combat operations on Negros.
June 3	1/511th PIR (+) para assault Camalaniugan, Luzon.
July 20	541st PIR absorbed into 11th Abn Div and 188th Glider Inf Regt redesignated 188th PIR.
August 12	11th Abn Div flown to Okinawa.
August 15	Japan declares intent to surrender (V-J Day).
August 30	11th Abn Div flown to Japan for occupation duty and remain until 1949.
September 2	Japan surrender.
December	503rd PIR depart for California.
December 25	503rd PIR inactivated at Camp Anza, CA.

CONSCRIPTION AND ENLISTMENT

Voluntary enlistment into the US army ceased on January 1, 1943. Most who had volunteered in the passionately patriotic days after Pearl Harbor had done so within three months. By the end of 1942, with the draft in full swing, there was little need for volunteers. However, if a man did not want to wait for his draft number to be drawn he could request his local draft board to put him on the list. Most of the men assigned to the 511th were conscripts, although they volunteered for the paratroopers. Most were 18 or 19 years old. The officers were not much older. The first commander of the 503rd, Colonel George M. Jones, was 32.

Military parachuting was a comparatively new concept and many did not know what "airborne"[2] meant. The first time that many heard about paratroopers was by reading a May 12, 1941, *LIFE Magazine* article and the exciting photographs inspired them to join. Paratrooper recruiting teams visited reception stations where both volunteer and drafted recruits reported. Young paratrooper sergeants screened records and selected physically fit men for interview. They told them what the paratroopers did and that they received $50 a month jump pay, doubling the pay of a Pfc. Officers received $100 to attract more to volunteer and because they performed jumpmaster duties (some NCOs were jumpmasters too with no pay increase). Many volunteers were enticed by the recruiters' paratrooper uniforms with their spit-shined jump boots, jaunty garrison cap, and silver jumpwings. Recruiting teams also visited infantry divisions undergoing training. Other recruits heard of the paratroopers by word of mouth and requested transfers. Many commanders refused to release bright, fit, proficient men and it took persistence to gain a transfer.

Prospective paratroopers were required to pass a flight physical and could not be color blind as they would need to determine the color of the red and green aircraft jump light and identify smoke and assembly panel colors. They needed an Army General Classification Test score of 110, the same as the score required for officers. Commanders were reluctant to let such men transfer because they were losing potential NCOs and lieutenants. Many volunteers did not realize the extent of the physical training they would have to endure. Some thought that by volunteering for the paratroopers they would simply undergo four weeks of jump training before being all set.

Posters such this one were instrumental in attracting young soldiers to the paratroopers. Paratroopers were required to be physically fit, between the ages of 18 and 32, between 5ft 6in. and 6ft 2in. tall, and to weigh under 185lb. (US Army)

Become a Paratrooper
☞ JUMP INTO THE FIGHT ☜

Soldiers between the ages of 18 and 32 inclusive, who believe they have the qualifications for this thrilling service, may apply for parachutist training. Ask your Commanding Officer for application form.

2 "Airborne" collectively defined parachute, glider, and specially trained troops landed by air transport.

TRAINING

The training of a parachute unit involved much more demanding preparation than its troops merely learning how to jump out of airplanes. Paratroopers were expected to be highly proficient in all required infantry skills, in superb physical condition, and highly motivated. Paratroopers were volunteers and as such they were expected to give their all and accept anything that was thrown at them. They could "un-volunteer" at any time if they so wished. They would then be reassigned to standard infantry units.

The 511th PIR was the tenth regiment raised. By the time it was activated in January 1943, the process of raising and training parachute regiments was highly refined. The regiment was organized at Camp Toccoa, GA[3] where two earlier regiments, the 506th and 501st PIRs, had trained; the 517th would later train there as well. The camp had been opened at the end of 1940 and was located four miles southwest of Toccoa in northeast Georgia. The 17,530-acre camp was a less than an ideal training area. The Toccoa Airport, which was six miles from the camp, was too short for a fully loaded transport to take off safely. This had already resulted in an earlier aircraft crash. The nearest rifle range was 30 miles to the northeast, at a military school range at Clemson Agricultural College in Clemson, South Carolina. There was, however, one local feature that units took advantage of. Currahee Mountain, 1,735ft above sea level and 800ft above the surrounding terrain, was southeast of the camp and was, as the saying goes, "three miles up and three miles down." A dirt road twisted and turned to the top, which was crowned by a fire lookout tower. In the base itself, the crude tarpaper two-squad hutments and pyramid tents housed 4,900 troops. Company headquarters, supply rooms, and other administrative buildings were the familiar "temporary" wood-frame buildings seen on most posts.

Some 12,000 recruits were screened for selection by the 511th and 3,000 were chosen. With an authorized strength of just over 2,000 men, the excess were expected to washout during the coming months' intensive training.

3 Originally named Camp Toombs, the commander of the 506th PIR had it changed to Camp Toccoa on August 21, 1942 as it was felt that "Toombs" was an inappropriate name for a paratrooper training camp, especially since the Toccoa Casket Company was nearby.

Camp Toccoa, GA, where the 511th PIR was activated and undertook its initial training. In the foreground are 16 x 16ft pyramidal squad tents. In the background are wood-frame and tarpaper squad hutments. (Currahee Military Museum, Toccoa, GA)

The suspended harness or "nut-cracker" was a less-than-comfortable exercise in which trainees were hung in a parachute harness and practiced "slips" by pulling down on the risers (connecting straps) to change the canopy's shape, forcing it to spill air and turn the parachute. Even with the minimal degree of "steering" that was possible, this maneuver allowed for an obstacle to be avoided and for the paratrooper to turn into the wind before landing. (US Army)

The cadre, the officers and NCO leaders, and the specialists were provided by the 505th PIR at Ft Benning, GA, the fourth parachute regiment raised. They assembled at Camp Toccoa in early January and prepared to receive volunteers from all over the country. It took days for all the volunteer, untrained conscripts to trickle in.

During the 47 days at Camp Toccoa the recruits undertook administrative processing, aptitude testing, job classification, uniform issue, inoculations, and physical and dental examinations. They learned how to wear their uniforms, make bunks, stow clothing and personal items in lockers, and set up inspection displays. They also learned the military ranks, whom to salute, and how to march in formation. At this point they had no weapons or equipment. There were a great many work details: receiving and storing supplies, grounds upkeep, police calls, kitchen police (KP), painting, and more. Every morning the physical fitness training began immediately after breakfast. Progressively longer runs and endless calisthenics were inflicted by screaming cadre sergeants and corporals. The cadres were not necessarily happy they had been selected. It meant they were reassigned from their original units, with which they had trained long and hard, separated from buddies, and were saddled with Mother Hubbarding a bunch of straight-leg recruits.

The recruits were impressed with the cadre which consisted of 250 soldiers who had been handpicked to provide the core of the new 511th. They were experienced NCOs filling the squad leader, platoon sergeant, and 1st sergeant slots. The cadre wore distinctive light brown paratrooper's uniforms with olive drab (OD) garrison caps bearing the parachutist's insignia, highly spit-shined jump boots, and silver jumpwings. It was not just the distinctive uniform that impressed, but the way these men carried themselves. They were obviously physically fit, confident, and knew what they were doing. They cut no slack, allowed no shortcuts, and demanded perfection in all tasks. The cadre included specialists such as supply sergeants, clerks, staff NCOs, vehicle and radio mechanics, radio operators, and wiremen, among others; all overseeing work details dealing with their area.

One of the most important actions undertaken at Camp Toccoa was classification and assignment. This required classification specialists to review each man's records and aptitude tests as well as to conduct interviews. They attempted to match up civilian skills and education with needed specialist skills. If no individual possessed the necessary skills for a specific role, a man interested in learning the job would be placed in said role. Of course, most positions simply required riflemen and weapons crewmen. Still, the men who were selected had a preference for machine guns or mortars. However, if there were no volunteers, soldiers were assigned to wherever they were needed.

Battalion and company commanders selected the men they wanted, sometimes competing over particular men. The cadre sergeant squad leaders selected the men they wanted as their future assistant corporals. The physical demands were great and men washed out every day. The War Department, based on inspector reports, wired the regimental commander stating that his selection process was too critical and ordering him to reduce the excessively high standards. By the time the telegram arrived it was too late. The process had run its course.

The physical training (PT) was the downfall of many of those who did not make the grade. Mornings were spent undertaking PT – all morning until dinner at noon. Even if there were other tasks and training to be accomplished, the minimum amount of exercise taken was the Army Daily Dozen. More often recruits would do repeated repetitions, sometimes after doing one- and two-mile runs for warm-up. The Daily Dozen consisted of the following:

1.	Side bender	7.	Flutter kick
2.	Toe touch	8.	Crunch
3.	Side straddle hop	9.	Lunger
4.	Windmill	10.	Knee bender
5.	Squat thrust	11.	Eight count push-up
6.	Six-inch leg lift	12.	Run in place

Throughout the day, during training, individuals or entire units could be instructed to drop and "Give me twenty-five!" push-ups for the slightest infractions. It could be for being the last man to complete a run or appearing not to pay full attention to instruction or for no apparent reason at all. Push-ups did not count if they were not executed correctly, that is, the shoulders, spine, backside, and legs kept perfectly straight, the arms extended fully in the up position and the chest touching the ground with each repetition. "One, two, three, four, four, four – 'bout time ya got it right, five … "

The runs were the toughest form of exercise. They were usually conducted after strenuous calisthenics which aimed to stretch the recruits, loosen them up, and get their wind up. Most runs were undertaken in platoon formation and run in step with NCOs shouting cadence chants. This made for a difficult run as the runner would have to stay in step and match the leader's pace and stride. The six-mile round trips up and down Currahee Mountain were brutal. Uphill was a long gradual climb on a seemingly endless rocky, dirt or mud road in service shoes and leggings. Downhill worked an entirely different set of muscles and stretched the insteps. To stress a platoon the leader might forgo the chants and allow the men to run in silence, letting them focus on their gasping pain. It would not take long for soldiers to start shouting for someone to "sing out," to lead them in chants to take their mind off their misery. What made the exercises, runs, and outdoor work worse was that the regiment's stay at Camp Toccoa was in midwinter, which meant they were often subjected to below-freezing temperatures, rain, and lots of mud. No one was exempt from PT and runs, be they private or colonel, or rifleman or staff NCO.

An early form of the swing-landing trainer; the improved type is under construction in the background. The trainee would be hoisted off the ground and swung in a manner similar to normal parachute oscillations. An instructor would release the trainee at some unexpected point allowing him to "land" when he should automatically execute a parachute landing fall in some unanticipated direction. (National Archives)

In the first weeks soldiers were detailed for KP and housekeeping work details, grounds upkeep, unloading supplies, etc. All were told, including officers, that if they decided to quit the paratroopers they had only to report to the orderly room and sign a washout slip. They were immediately reassigned to Company W – "washout." Officers were reassigned to straight-leg infantry units. Company W troops were issued blue denim fatigues and assigned all the KP and work details allowing the remaining paratroopers to train without distractions. Another benefit of this was that the humiliated blue denim-clad washouts motivated the troops not to quit. The 511th did not train alone. It was joined by the 457th Prcht FA Bn on February 21, 1943. Like the 511th it had been activated on January 5, but at Ft Bragg. The artillerymen completed their selection with the 511th.

By the time the 511th departed for Camp Mackall the regiment numbered about 2,000 enlisted, 173 officers, and three warrant officers. At the time the regiment was authorized 140 officers, five warrant officers and 1,884 enlisted, totaling 2,029.

The 34ft tower has been called the "great separator." Trainees made a vigorous exit to experience the sensation of exiting an aircraft. They slid down a 200ft cable to a mound. After their initial tower jumps they made others with the aim of practicing opening a reserve parachute. (National Archives)

Training the regiment

On March 21, 1943, the 511th PIR arrived by train at Camp Mackall, NC[4]. Four days later the regiment was officially assigned to the 11th Abn Div which was activated on February 25, 1943, with a cadre of several hundred officers and men. Ft Bragg, the home of Airborne Command, abutted Camp Mackall. When activated, the division lacked not only its paratroopers, but also all of its non-parachute units, including its two glider regiments, two glider artillery battalions, and the many support units. From January into March, thousands of fillers arrived from all over the country to be assigned to the blossoming units. As well as a few paratroopers assigned to some of the support units, one of the engineer battalion's companies was also parachute, for example; these troops were not volunteers. Some requested a transfer when they learned they would ride in gliders.

The future paratroopers considered themselves somewhat above the arriving recruits, who did not yet have parachutist uniforms. They may not have been paratroopers yet, but they were an organized unit, had made it through the grueling selection at Camp Toccoa, and felt like vets compared with the confused recruits.

The already organized and manned 511th PIR and 457th Prcht FA Bn were assigned secluded barracks in the camp's west end. They continued training and were issued weapons and equipment. The PT and runs did not decrease and forced marches were undertaken by all. These "rat races" gradually increased in length up to 25 miles. Another phenomenon emerged – the "Swing Session."

4 Opened in January 1943, the 56,000-acre post was named Camp Hoffman after the nearby railroad station until it was renamed on February 8 after Pvt. John T. Mackall (1920–42), the first paratrooper killed in combat near Oran, Algeria with 2/503rd PIR.

With Major General Joseph M. Swing (1894–1984) and the division's two brigadier generals leading the formation of every officer in the division, they conducted frequent and lengthy runs, terminating at the hated obstacle course, and then adjourned to the beer hall ("slop chute"). It was Swing's way of ensuring officers met the same standards as the troops and of bonding them.

With the regiment organized, leaders assigned, and weapons and equipment issued, they commenced 17 weeks of parachute infantry training in which every man learned his job as well as the skills needed by all soldiers regardless of job. The cadre NCO leaders and specialists presented the training. Platoons were kept together, but specialists from different companies – radio operators, mechanics, draftsmen, clerks, etc. – were grouped together for training.

When it came to infantry training, the rifle platoons' platoon sergeant, the two rifle squad and one mortar squad leaders had been through the entire training cycle in their former units. It was their job to train their platoon. The one or two lieutenants assigned to the platoon might command the platoon, but most were fresh from Officer Candidate School – "90-day wonders" – and they had as much to learn as their charges.

Infantry training covered a wide range of individual and small-unit skills. The weather was generally mild, but spring rains were frequent, the nights were chilly, and there was plenty of mud. Speed marches were conducted frequently and included marching to the field for training and to firing ranges. Many of the ranges were located at Ft Bragg, a considerable distance away via Chicken and Plank Roads. Marches ranged from two miles at the double-time to 32 miles in eight hours, always with full equipment including overcoat, raincoat, extra boots, rations, etc., all interspersed with the Army Daily Dozen. The troops ran obstacle, bayonet, and live-fire infiltration courses. The latter entailed low crawling out of a trench *toward* three or four machine guns firing over their heads. There were barbed wire obstacles and demolition pits. The crack of bullets, streaking tracers, showering dirt from the explosions, and crawling through mud beneath barbed wire gave the troops a brief taste of combat. There was also the new close-combat course which entailed quick-reaction firing at surprise pop-up targets while crossing broken terrain and obstacles with an emphasis on speed and accuracy. Two weeks of continuous field exercises were required. This was when small-unit tactics were practiced.

There were a multitude of new subjects to learn and become proficient in. Skills common to all jobs included:

Subject	Hours
Military courtesy and discipline, Articles of War	6
Orientation course	7
Military sanitation, first aid, and sex hygiene	10
Defense against chemical attack, individual	12
Practice marches and bivouacs (min. hours)	20
Dismounted drill	20
Equipment, clothing, and shelter tent pitching	7
Interior guard duty	4
Hasty field fortifications and camouflage	8
Elementary map and aerial photo reading (min. hours)	8
Physical training (min. hours)	36
Inspections	18
Protection of military information	3
Organization of the Army	1

Training was conducted on all of the platoon's weapons: rifle, carbine submachine gun, pistol, light machine gun, mortar, and hand and rifle grenades. They learned how to lay and remove antitank and antipersonnel mines, basic demolitions, bayonet use, hand-to-hand combat, field fortifications, tactical camouflage, land navigation, compass use, arm and hand signals, individual movement techniques, patrolling, scouting, and squad, platoon and company tactics. The training was tough. One soldier reported, "Our non-coms said the training would make us so ornery we'd be able to chew razor blades and spit nails."

Since they would go into combat as a platoon they learned a great deal about one another and developed tight teamwork. They knew what their buddies' profiles looked like at night and recognized their movements, they knew what to expect from one another, who had the best abilities in certain jobs, and who the real leaders were.

Jump school
With infantry training under their belts and a high degree of unit *esprit de corps* established, the 511th faced its next challenge. They journeyed to Ft Benning for three weeks of jump training, from mid-May to mid-June 1943. Instruction was divided into four week-long phases. Stage "A" was skipped as they had undertaken more than the required PT preparation.

The 250ft towers at Ft Benning, GA. Three trainees are being hoisted to the top before being released to drift freely ("freefall") into a vast sawdust-covered area. Three other trainees on the far tower to the left have just been released under their special 32ft J-1 canopies. Trainees typically made several tower jumps. Depending on wind direction, between one and three trainees would be dropped at a time. The three freefall towers are still in use today. The far tower is a controlled jump tower and is no longer in use. (Tom Laemlein, Armor Plate Press)

Stage "B" involved door exits (mock door); suspended harness training with canopy slipping ("steering"); oscillation checking; hazardous landing training; use of the swing landing trainer to learn body position during landing; tumbling exercises; and endlessly jumping off 2ft, 3ft and 5ft platforms into sawdust pits to practice landing attitude.

Stage "C" concentrated on the controlled jump tower, a 34ft high tower with C-47 exit doors. The students jumped out assuming the correct body position and slid down a declined 200ft cable. They also undertook several jumps from the two 250ft free towers. Cables hoisted jumpers up under a parachute held open by a ring. They were released and learned to guide the parachute to the ground and practice actual landing falls. Two tower jumps were made at night. They also had to learn how to deflate a canopy while being dragged by the wind, which could be a hazardous operation. There were no quick-release fittings allowing the canopy to be released from the harness to deflate it. They had to be able to scramble to their feet, run ahead of the bellowing canopy, and spill the air out of it by violently pulling the suspension lines. If the wind were strong enough and the paratrooper not nimble enough he might not be able to run past the canopy to spill the air and might be yanked off his feet.

Stage "D" was the five qualification jumps from C-47 transports. The first jumps were individual tap-outs followed by mass exits with all jumpers exiting as fast as they could. The last jump was with combat equipment. Not a single

A trainee is suspended beneath the "pre-opened" special 32ft J-2 canopy used on the 250ft controlled jump tower. The canopy remained attached to the hoist and guide cables. Contrary to popular opinion, these towers were not used at the 1939–40 New York World's Fair. The controlled drop tower there had 12 arms and was moved to Coney Island in 1941, where it still stands inoperable. (Tom Laemlein, Armor Plate Press)

511th soldier refused to jump once aboard the aircraft. Owing to their extended physical training and ground training, jump injuries were minimal. Most of the new paratroopers found that their most difficult jump was their second or third as they hadn't known what to expect during the first.

They were paratroopers now and able to don paratroopers' suits, paratroopers' garrison caps, jump boots, and the most prized possession of all – their silver wings which were pinned on after they assembled on the DZ.

 JUMP SCHOOL

Both the 503rd and 511th undertook their initial jump training at the Ft Benning Parachute School. Later, they both ran their own jump schools modeled after that of Ft Benning. All they lacked was the 250ft tower which, while beneficial, was not absolutely necessary. The units conducted their own jump schools as it was necessary to train the continuously arriving fillers and replacements, who were not always jump-trained. There was a constant stream of these soldiers owing to troops being reassigned as cadres or volunteering for OCS and other courses, and also because of the need to replace injured and ill personnel, and combat losses. The 503rd ran a jump school at Camp Cable at Gordonvale, Australia. The 511th operated schools at DeRidder Army Airfield, LA; Buna-Dobodura in Papua New Guinea and, after the war, at Yanome and then Carolus Field in Japan.

Paratroopers learned the necessary skills on a number of training apparatus which are still used today in improved form. The C-47 transport mockup (**1**) taught jumpers pre-jump procedures inside the aircraft and how to exit. On the suspended harness trainer or "nut-cracker" (**2**) they learned, albeit uncomfortably, how to pull slips and maneuver the parachute, somewhat. On the jump platforms (**3**), some angled from 3–5ft and others 5ft high, they learned how to execute parachute landing falls by jumping and rolling into sawdust pits. The swing landing trainer (**4**) saw the jumpers in a suspended harness that swung in a way similar to an osculating or drifting parachute giving them the opportunity to learn how to anticipate the direction and angle of landing. Students awaiting their turn (**5**) in the 34ft tower observed students making exits, both good and poor, and learned from their example. The 34ft tower (**6**) was called the "separator" as it separated the willing from the unwilling. It taught jumpers how to make a proper and strong exit and they experienced a degree of "opening shock." They slid on trolleys down a 200ft cable to a mound. At the mound (**7**) waiting students unhooked the "rope jumpers" and ran the trolleys, which were fastened to a towrope, back to the tower. Quonset huts (**8**) housed the instructors' break room, equipment storage, and aid station. The self-propelled Wincharger wind-machine (**9**) blew inflated canopies with a prone student attached across the ground allowing said student to scramble to his feet and run around the blowing canopy attempting to turn it into the wind and collapse it. Students were organized into platoons of four 10–14-man "sticks" (**10**), a stick being the jumpers loaded into a single transport.

The next day they received their jump school certificates. By this time paratroopers no longer packed their own chutes so, at the same time, parachute packers were being trained. Parachutes were packed and maintained by the new parachute maintenance company. Packing required too much training time and detracted from the paratroopers' tactical training. Also, the paratroopers would not be as proficient as dedicated packers.

Unit training

It was a cocky regiment that returned to Camp Mackall for unit training. They were soon back in the pine forests undertaking platoon training and tests, more live-fire courses, and then company exercises. Practice jumps were made frequently, beginning with squad, then platoon, and then company jumps. All jumps were always followed by some form of tactical exercise. Jumps were made in daylight, at twilight, and at night. In July they conducted ten-day tactical bivouacs and then conducted battalion jumps and exercises.

In the fall of 1943, a controversy regarding the future of the airborne divisions emerged. The marginal performance of airborne units in North Africa and Sicily led to recommendations that the divisions be disbanded and only parachute battalions be employed. To test the validity of the airborne and look for solutions to problem areas, the Knollwood Maneuvers took place on December 6–11. The reinforced 11th Abn Div served as the attackers against a reinforced 17th Abn Div regiment. The demanding exercise, made more difficult by bad weather, proved a success and the airborne units were preserved. It was also a very good training experience for the 511th.

Upon its return to Camp Mackall and Christmas and New Year's celebrations, the division was alerted to move to Ft Polk, LA, with the new year. There they would conduct final exercises and prepare for overseas movement. Twenty-two troop trains moved the division to Ft Polk. Unit training continued, along with a series of three-day exercises and individual and unit tests in the Calcasieu swamps. The weather was cold, accompanied by much rain. The division ran exercises from squad through to regimental level, approach marches, attacks, defenses, and withdrawals. A jump school was set up at DeRidder Army Air Field, 17 miles to the southwest. Major General Swing's goal was to make his regiments dual capable – parachute and glider.

Douglas C-47D transports. The Skytrain or "Gooney Bird" of Troop Carrier Command was the mainstay jump aircraft. The only jump door was on the left side. Note it has a double door, but for troop jumping the forward half of the door was removed. (National Archives)

A posed publicity photo of a paratrooper with a .45-cal M1 Thompson submachine gun. While 28ft C-4 canopies for the T-5 troop parachute used In combat were camouflage-patterned, C-3 white models were used in training and sometimes seen in combat. (National Archives)

Many glidermen undertook parachute training, but were not given jump pay or distinctive uniforms and insignia.

When in the cantonment areas, the barracks and entertainment facilities on Polk were better than those offered at Mackall. Polk, however, was an armor training post and there was a great deal of rivalry with the tankers. Diversion off-post left a great deal to be desired.

The unit had been informed that it would depart for overseas deployment on March 15. All personnel underwent clothing and equipment serviceability inspections and all paperwork was updated. The departure was delayed by a month, which was filled with more training. The division began boarding trains on April 20, 1944, and by the 28th the entire division had arrived at Camp Stoneman, CA.

Rank

Recruits were quickly taught the nuances of Army rank. Privates and privates first class were collectively called and addressed as "privates." They displayed

PARATROOPER, 1943

(1) and (2) depict a rifleman wearing a T-5 troop parachute assembly with his disassembled M1 rifle in a Griswold container fastened to his right side. He wears tan unlined horsehide riding gloves (3), which were standard issue to paratroopers. The equipment displayed includes the front (4) and back (5) of the T-5 reserve parachute, the back of the Griswold container (6) with the fastening snaphook, the front of the submachine container (7) for Thompsons or the grease gun (Thompsons could also be carried in the Griswold container), and the B-4 pneumatic life preserver vest or "Mae West" (8). The two-chamber vest could be inflated by two 0.280oz CO_2 cylinders or by two backup oral inflation tubes. The B-4 was introduced in mid-1942 and replaced the similar, but more complicated to manufacture, B-3. It was mandatory for life vests to be worn under the parachute harness, but over individual web gear, when the flight route passed over large bodies of water. A jumper descending into water ensured his rear end was firmly seated in the harness seat, unfastened his reserve letting it swing to the left side, unfastened the chest then leg straps, and clamped his arms tightly to his sides to stay in the harness. When his feet hit the water he threw his arms up, slid out of the harness, pulled the two CO_2 pull-cords, and swam upwind or up-current away from the parachute canopy and entangling suspension lines. The vest was sufficient to keep the jumper afloat with all his equipment.

4

5

3

1

8

6

2

7

a "slick sleeve" and a single point-up chevron, respectively. Soldiers joked that Pfc meant "praying for corporal." Privates who wore no rank insignia, were often referred to as "buck privates."

NCOs – "noncoms" – were corporals and up and held leadership and supervisory positions. A corporal, an "entry level" NCO, was commonly known as "corp," "two-striper," or "jack." Next in line was the sergeant, "a three-striper," or "buck sergeant" to differentiate him from the higher sergeant grades identified by a suffix. This was followed by staff sergeant identified by three chevrons and a rocker. The next grade up was technical sergeant, "tech sergeant," identified by two rockers. Prior to September 1942 first sergeants were in the same pay grade (grade 2) as tech sergeants and wore the same chevrons, but with a diamond added. In that September they were moved up to pay grade 1, with three rockers and a diamond. The first sergeant was the senior NCO in a company and responsible for unit administration and overseeing all enlisted men. Master sergeant – "three up and three down" or a "six-striper" – was the senior NCO rank. These men filled battalion "sergeant major" positions and staff NCO slots in higher headquarters. It should be noted that the American "sergeant major" bore no semblance to the all-powerful British sergeant-major or today's US command sergeant major. The World War II sergeant major was an administrative assistant to the battalion adjutant. All sergeants were addressed simply as "sergeant" and informally as "sarge." Some, however, discouraged the use of the latter.

In January 1942 a new rank category was introduced, leading to some confusion. The three "technician" ranks replaced the "private specialist." Specialists were Pfcs, but received higher pay grades. They officially wore a Pfc chevron and no other identification, but in some units prior to the war they were locally authorized one to six rockers which corresponded to their pay grade. In other words, a specialist six might wear six rockers and was paid the same as a master sergeant, but had no supervisory authority. With the expansion of the Army in 1940 the use of rockers by specialists disappeared.

The new technicians at first wore the same chevrons as corporals, sergeants, and staff sergeants. In September 1942 a "T" was added to their chevrons. Authority-wise the tech 5 fell below corporal, and tech 4 and 3 below a buck sergeant. Most units treated them no differently from NCOs in the same pay grade. They might be addressed as a "tech 5" or "T/5," but they were more commonly addressed simply as corporal or sergeant, their equivalent, pay-wise, NCO ranks. While they held no leadership positions, techs, regardless of grade, could be assigned as an assistant squad leader in lieu of a corporal if necessary.

The term "acting jack" was applied to both acting corporals and sergeants. "Jack" was a corporal so it may have been interpreted as a Pfc acting as a corporal or a corporal acting as a sergeant, a "jawbone corporal."

This M1A1 carbine-armed master sergeant carries a brown leather M17 binocular case, civilian hunting knife, lightweight service gasmask case, and a 33ft parachutist rope that would allow him to climb out of a tree if he landed in one. (Tom Laemlein, Armor Plate Press)

The term "Hollywood private" also referred to an acting corporal or a Pfc awaiting promotion to corporal.

In regard to rifle company duty positions, squad leaders were sergeants, assistant squad leaders were corporals, and platoon sergeants were staff sergeants. These positions were increased one grade in December 1943.

APPEARANCE AND EQUIPMENT

Paratroopers' uniforms

Paratroopers were issued with the popular "parachute jumper's" uniform. It consisted of a thigh-length coat with a zippered front opening and snap-closed breast and skirt pockets. The pockets were the bellows type. The angled breast pockets allowed easier access. The coat included an integral cloth waist belt. The trousers had front internal pockets and large bellows-type cargo pockets on the sides. The trousers were tapered to allow easy blousing into jump boots. The suit was made of lightweight wind-resistant and water-repellent cotton. It was light brown in color, a darker brownish shade than khaki. Suspenders were often worn under the coat, but the M1937 OD web waist belt with a brass square open-face buckle was usually used. This belt was also used with the fatigue trousers. The 503rd wore them on New Guinea, but they were soon replaced. This good-looking uniform went on to influence the Vietnam-era jungle fatigues and the 1980s battledress uniform. However, it proved ill-suited for the tropics. Being made from a tight-weave fabric, it was too hot and its light weight did not hold up well in the jungle. Also, its brownish shade provided inadequate camouflage.

Far more practical in the tropics were the standard herringbone twill fatigue jacket and trousers, which were made of tough hard-wearing cotton. While not ideal – they were slow to dry and were fairly warm – they allowed better air circulation than the paratrooper's uniform. They also benefited from being a dark green color which provided good camouflage. They faded to a lighter gray-green following exposure to the sun and laundering, but this was still better than the paratrooper suit's brown color. The hip-length jacket was worn out of the trousers for better air circulation. It had a button-closed front opening and patch pockets, large enough for a K-ration meal, on the breasts. Early issue trousers had large internal "bag" pockets which resulted in heat traps, causing them to bunch up and stay damp after the rest of the uniform had dried. Later issue trousers had large external cargo pockets on the upper thighs. Some troops preferred the one-piece herringbone twill work suit during training and it was sometimes worn in combat. The "mechanic's coveralls" had an integral cloth belt. As it was a one-piece, this outfit was warmer and had to be almost completely removed in order to relieve oneself. It had a large patch pocket on the left breast and large pockets of the upper thighs. A lightweight OD knit wool sweater was available. These were worn at night, even in the tropics.

Headgear included the M1C paratrooper's steel helmet and liner, the short-visored herringbone twill fatigue cap, and the cotton khaki or wool OD garrison cap. The steel helmet and liner were lusterless dark OD.

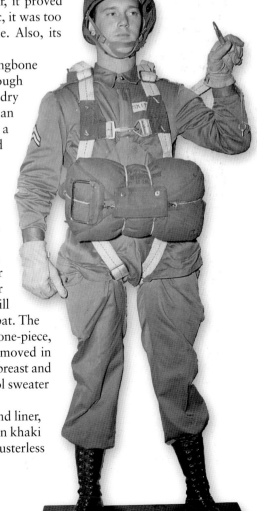

This corporal wears the M1942 parachutist uniform and M2 parachutist helmet. He holds his static line snaphook in the ready position to hook it to the aircraft's anchor line cable. The snaphook's retaining pin can be seen dangling from a cord. He wears no combat equipment of any kind and as such is rigged to make a "Hollywood jump." Note the black on white name tag on his left chest, a practice adopted by some units, but seldom seen overseas. (Tom Laemlein, Armor Plate Press)

Major General Joseph M. Swing, Commanding General, 11th Abn Div, briefs his staff in front of a 16 x 33ft M1942 squad tent used as a CP. The staff frequently wore khakis in the rear areas. (Tom Laemlein, Armor Plate Press)

White and OD cotton undershirts and under drawers were issued. In the tropics undergarments were seldom worn as they retained sweat in the underarms and crotch and this resulted in rashes – "jungle rot." OD or light gray cotton and wool cushion sole socks or "boot socks" were issued. The toe, sole, and heel were made from double-thick material.

Paratroopers' uniform distinctions

Paratroopers possessed a number of uniform distinctions which set them apart from their earthbound counterparts. With extra money in their pockets they often had their uniforms, whether khakis or wool OD Class A service uniforms, precisely tailored beyond the tailoring supplied by the quartermaster. It was the paratroopers' uniform that attracted so many recruits as much as anything else. Paratroopers did not wear the peaked service cap or "bus driver's cap." They wore only the garrison cap, known as the "overseas cap" or "c**t cap."

 PARATROOPER SERVICE UNIFORMS

The corporal (**1**) wears the wool serge service uniform with the OD wool paratrooper's cap. The collar brass consists of a U.S. on the right collar and the infantry crossed rifles on the left. The Overseas Service Bar on the left cuff represents six months' service in a combat zone and was authorized in 1944, but retroactive to the war's beginning. The cotton khaki service uniform is worn by the pfc (**2**) along with a cotton khaki paratrooper's cap. Both paratroopers wear bloused Cochran jump boots. The insert insignia includes the shoulder sleeve insignia of the 11th Abn Div (**3**), and the unofficial pocket patches and jumpwing ovals of the 503rd (**4a** and **4b**) and 511th (**5a** and **5b**) Parachute Infantry Regiments. These were mainly worn by officers on flight jackets, which were little needed in the tropics and fell out of use. In the States, and even overseas when assigned to Sixth or Eighth Armies, the 503rd often wore the Airborne Command patch (**6**). A 511th PIR paratrooper without any decorations for valor, but having been wounded in combat in this case, would typically possess the decorations in this ribbon bar (**7**). Ribbons are described from the viewer's upper left to lower right. The Parachutist Badge with 511th PIR background oval, Bronze Star Medal, Purple Heart (second award), Asiatic-Pacific Campaign Medal with three Campaign Stars, World War II Victory Medal, Army of Occupation Medal, Philippine Liberation Medal (issued by the Commonwealth of the Philippines), and the coveted Combat Infantryman's Badge (**8**). The Army of Occupation Medal ribbon is displayed reversed ("upside down"). It was wrongly assumed that if occupying Japan the red was worn to the left and black to the left if in Germany, the latter was the actual correct manner regardless of country.

3

5a

7

8

6

4b

4a

5b

ANGELS 511th

1

2

This was edged with braid in the enlisted men's branch of service color, robin's egg blue (light blue) for the infantry and red for artillery and engineers. Officers wore gold and black braid, warrant officers silver and black, and general officers gold. The overseas cap had been replaced by the campaign hat after World War I, but was retained by the Air Corps. In July 1940 the Parachute Test Platoon was issued khaki garrison caps to wear with the one-piece mechanic's coveralls they wore in training. As the airborne troops expanded, the garrison cap, with the addition of the airborne cap insignia, became the paratroopers' cap. It was worn with field uniforms in training and in rear areas, a practice not undertaken by non-airborne units when the cap began to be issued Army-wide.

The first insignia adopted by the airborne, the parachute patch, was sewn one inch from the left front of the garrison cap's curtain. For the infantry this was a light blue disc with a white parachute canopy and border. Artillery units had a red disc and other units the blue or red, whichever was the closest to their branch color. (Units designated glider wore a similar patch depicting a glider and airborne units wore one with both a glider and parachute even though they were not parachute qualified.) The patch was large enough for a silver dollar to be sewn under it. This provided emergency funds – a dollar could buy a lot – added weight to the cap to make it sit firmly at a jaunty angle, and in a bar altercation provided a surprisingly hearty wallop in an antagonist's face (it weighed 26.73 grams – almost an ounce). Officers wore the parachute patch on the right front with their rank pinned on the left. It was not uncommon for enlisted men to sew it on the right side by mistake. Even though this was the standard Army-wide garrison cap, with the addition of the parachute patch it was commonly called the "paratrooper's cap."

The coveted Parachutist Badge or "jumpwings" was the most distinctive of the paratrooper's insignia. It was approved in March 1941. The silver wings were worn on the left chest above the pocket. "Jumpwing ovals," embroidered backings, were worn by parachute infantry units[5]. The 511th's had a light green center, white inner border, and a dark green outer border. The 503rd's was red with a wide silver-gray border.

The 511th PIR wore the 11th Abn Div patch – a blue shield bearing a red disc with white wings and a white "11." The crowning Airborne Tab was white on blue worn ½in. below the left shoulder seam. The tab was worn by all members of the division whether they were parachute qualified or not. It was a unit insignia and had nothing to do with individual qualifications. There was a little-used unofficial 511th pocket patch, a blue disc with a white parachute and a goofy-looking, halo-crowned dog behind an "8 ball" with his tongue hanging out. The patch was inscribed "511th ANGLES."

One of the most noticeable and most jealously guarded paratrooper distinctions were paratrooper boots, or jump boots. Corcoran boots were high-topped (10in.), capped-toe boots with thick soles designed for maximum ankle support. They were dark brown, kept highly spit-shined, and worn with the trouser bloused (tucked) into the boot tops. Because of the bloused nature of trousers worn with the boots, non-jumpers wearing straight-legged trousers were commonly referred to as "straight-legs." Because of their bloused trousers paratroopers were referred to as having "baggy pants." It was not uncommon for "legs" to privately purchase

5 Jumpwing ovals were not officially recognized until 1949 and not entered into uniform regulations until 1957 when they were designated "airborne background trimmings."

A carbine-armed bazooka man fires a 2.36in. M9 rocket launcher at a Japanese position. He wears a khaki Swing cap. (Tom Laemlein, Armor Plate Press)

Corcorans and wear them while on pass. Tankers and MPs did the same. This was seldom tolerated by paratroopers and they would quickly gang up, remove the boots from offenders, and with a rigger's knife quickly convert them to low-quarters, sometimes without first removing them. The staff of the 82nd Abn Div, who were not required to be parachute-qualified, were allowed to wear jump boots if they made one parachute jump (but they received no jumpwings). The 505th PIR was not impressed and issued a notice that any paratrooper making a single glider landing could wear shoes and leggings. Jump boots provided good support, but were heavy and on Leyte it was found they were not waterproof enough.

In late 1944 paratroopers began to be issued the russet brown M1943 combat service boots which were issued to all troops. This was not a popular move. They had a two-buckle flap at the top and it was possible for this to snag on parachute suspension lines during a poor tumbling exit. They also did not provide sufficient ankle support. Many paratroopers ceased wearing Corcorans in the field to preserve them for wear with service uniforms.

The so-called "Swing cap" was not an official part of the uniform. It was designed by the 11th Abn Div's Gen Swing and styled after a railroader's cap. Photographic evidence shows some members of the 503rd also donned the Swing cap. It was a visored field cap with a large full crown which made it cooler than other caps. It was made in Australia from both khaki uniform cloth and light OD cotton. It was often worn without insignia, but officers might wear their rank on the front. Many wore a white-on-blue Airborne Tab on the front and/or the circular white-on-blue parachute patch on the right or left side.

Weapons

Paratroopers used the same weapons as ground-pounding infantrymen, but they were somewhat differently allocated.

When the 511th was issued with its M1 rifles and carbines the guns were brand new, packed in cosmoline. After hours of cleaning, the soldiers found themselves fully coated with the brown, oily, waxy gunk with no appreciable reduction of the substance on their weapons.

The semi-automatic .30-cal Garand M1 was the standard infantry rifle and proved extremely robust. For parachute jumping, the Garand was broken down into three component groups: the barrel and receiver group, the stock, and the trigger housing group. This allowed it to be packed in a smaller container. Sometimes, it would be rolled up in a parachute kit bag and strapped behind the reserve parachute or strapped to the side of the parachute harness in a padded Griswold container. It could be reassembled in less than 15 seconds, including unpacking.

The earlier raised 503rd was initially issued some .30-cal Springfield M1903 rifles, one per squad for the grenadier. It was a bolt-action, five-shot rifle and could be fitted with an M1 grenade launcher. In late 1943, the M7 grenade launcher became available for the M1 rifle and the Springfields were replaced. However, the M7 launcher prevented the Garand from being fired semi-automatically when fitted.

The .30-cal M1A1 carbine was a folding-stock version of the wooden-stocked M1. Its tubular steel stock folded to the left and was a quarter-pound heavier than the wooden stock. The M1A1 was originally intended only for parachute engineers, but extended to parachute infantry and artillery. Its production ceased in mid-1944 and it was replaced by the M1A3 carbine. This had a more robust pantographic-stamped steel stock that folded underneath. It saw limited issue in early 1945. Carbines had 15-round magazines. Carbines used a smaller round than rifles and machine guns and provided poor accuracy at over 150 yards, along with poor penetration and knockdown power. Many 511th riflemen used carbines on Leyte, where ranges were short, but their poor penetration and problems with mud caused them to fall out of favor. They also proved ineffectual when used in house-to-house fighting on Manila. Some complained that the gun sounded like a Japanese 6.5mm rifle, which sometimes caused it to draw friendly fire. During a jump, folding stock carbines were carried in a canvas scabbard attached to the parachute harness. In 1944, the mortar squad was authorized M1A1 carbines in lieu of M1 rifles. However, as the mortarmen were frequently required to act as riflemen, it appears

D PARATROOPER WEAPONS

With the exception of the folding stock M1A1 carbine, paratroopers used the same weapons as the straight-leg infantry. The M1A1 carbine (**4**) used a 15-round magazine and fired a much smaller .30-cal round than the M1 rifle, BAR, and machine guns. It lies on the carbine leg scabbard. The .30-cal M1 Garand rifle (**1**) was used by most riflemen and is here fitted with an M7 grenade launcher. For carrying while jumping, the M1 could be broken down into three components and stored inside the padded Griswold container (**3**). The .30-cal M1903 Springfield rifle (**7**) was used with the M1 grenade launcher until late 1943, when the M7 was available for the Garand. The M1 used an eight-round clip and the M1903 a five-round stripper clip. The .30-cal M1918A2 BAR (**8**) was not standard issue, but often replaced the squad light machine gun. The BAR's bipod was often removed, as here, to reduce weight and the carrying handle was not retro-fitted until near the war's end. The BAR had a 20-round magazine. The .45-cal M1 and M1A1 Thompson submachine guns (**5**) were used until the end of the war and were supplemented in late 1944 with the .45-cal M3 "grease gun" (**6**). Both had 30-round magazines, but of different design. The earlier M1928A1 Thompson (not shown) remained in use throughout the war, but used a 20-round magazine. The .45-cal M1911A1 Colt pistol (**2**) used a seven-round magazine. The .30-cal M1919A4 light machine gun (**9**), with a 250-round ammunition can, equipped rifle squads and regimental machine gun platoons. Each rifle platoon had one 2.36in. M1A1 antitank rocket launcher or bazooka (**10**). The M6 rocket bag was modified for paratrooper use by adding a V-ring, snaphook, and leg tie-down straps on the back.

1

3

2

4

5

6

7

8

9

CAL .30M1
AMMUNITION BOX

10

most of them retained their rifles because of their superior firepower.

On paper, all paratroopers in rifle companies were issued with .45-cal Colt M1911A1 pistols. Many opted not to carry them or they were simply not issued with them. However, there appeared to be sufficient numbers if a man wanted one. The rugged and reliable "forty-five" used a seven-round magazine of which three were issued per pistol. The authority to issue them to all paratroopers was withdrawn in February 1944.

Limited use was made of the .45-cal Thompson M1928A1 submachine guns with 20-round magazines. They began to be replaced in 1943 by the improved Thompson M1 and M1A1 versions with a 30-round magazine (it could accept the earlier 20-round magazine as well). Some M1928A1s remained in use. In late 1944, some .45-cal M3 "grease guns" were issued, with a different 30-round magazine.

The most common complaint made about the M1 rifle was that it was somewhat heavy. However, its ruggedness and reliability very much countered this complaint. Complaints about the M1 carbine were numerous and most members of the rifle platoons preferred Garands. The primary complaints made about the Thompsons were about their weight and poor penetration through dense jungle foliage.

Parachute units were not issued with the .30-cal M1918A2 Browning automatic rifle, which was normally issued one per squad. Instead, each rifle squad was provided with two .30-cal Browning M1919A4 light machine guns. There was one dedicated crew and a spare gun for defensive use. It appears the spares were little, if ever, used. Battalion light machine gun platoons were also equipped with the air-cooled, tripod-mounted, 250-round, belt-fed guns. However, the 503rd and 511th PIR often replaced the 44lb machine guns with Browning Automatic Rifles (BARs). The BAR was heavy and temperamental. A major flaw was the 20-round magazine which made it

Paratroopers check their equipment prior to boarding their aircraft. Here, an M1 Garand rifle is slung reversed, muzzle down on the jumper's left side and secured under the reserve parachute's belly band by his elbow. It was also jumped in the same manner on the right side or packed in a padded Griswold container (a parachutist's rifle holster assembly) on one side or the other or between the reserve and the chest. (US Army)

During Stateside training, a paratrooper wearing a Type B-3 inflatable life vest for safety reasons prepares a demolition charge on an "enemy" bridge. He is armed with an M1 carbine. Many parachute units did not receive the folding stock M1A1 until they deployed overseas. (Tom Laemlein, Armor Plate Press)

impossible to maintain sustained supporting fire. The brush-catching 2½lb bipod was often removed to reduce the 19⅖lb total weight. The water-cooled .30-cal Browning M1917A1 heavy machine gun was not used by the paratroopers.

The 60mm M2 mortar, while a company weapon in ground units, was a platoon weapon for the airborne troops. The 42lb weapon could be broken down into three loads: barrel – 12⅘lb, bipod – 16⅖lb, baseplate – 12⅘lb. Its range was 1,985yds with a minimum range of 100yds.

The 2.36in. M1A1 rocket launcher or "bazooka" proved to be an effective lightweight antitank weapon that saw much use against pillboxes, bunkers, field fortifications, caves, and buildings. Its range was 250yds, but it was more effective at under 100yds. It weighed only 13⅕lb, but was 54½in. long making

Not yet parachute-trained, two future paratroopers examine a .45-cal M1928A1 Thompson submachine gun with a 20-round magazine. These guns were later replaced with simplified M1 and M1A1 Thompsons and later still by M3 "grease guns," all with 30-round magazines. (National Archives)

it awkward to jump with. Its muzzle and breech would be wrapped with padding and the launcher would be slung vertically on the jumper's side. In late 1944, the much-improved M9 bazooka was fielded. It had a slightly longer range, weighed 15.87lb, and was 61in. long. This additional length was not a hindrance during jumps as it could be broken down into two sections with a length of 31½in., making it easy to jump with.

Hand grenades included the Mk II and Mk IIA1 fragmentation, Mk IIIA1 and Mk IIIA2 concussion, M15 white phosphorus (WP), M16 and M18 colored smoke, and AN-M8 white smoke. Rifle grenades were the M9A1 antitank, M17 fragmentation, M19 white phosphorus, and various colored smoke and flares for signaling and target marking. There were also rifle grenade adaptors – tailboom and fin assemblies – to which frag and smoke hand grenades could be fitted and launched as rifle grenades.

Riflemen carried the 16in. M1905 or M1942 bayonet. From 1943, 10in. M1905E1 and M1 bayonets were issued. All four of these could be fixed to M1 and M1903 rifles. The M2 pocketknife had a 3⅛in. switchblade and was carried by paratroopers to cut lines that had become entangled on landing. While prohibited, paratroopers often carried their switchblades on pass. The M3 fighting knife had a 6¾in. blade. They were issued to those without a bayonet, but other paratroopers managed to obtain them. Issue began in early 1943. It provided the basis for the later M4 bayonet for the carbine, itself not issued until the war's end. Some men were issued with the M1918 Mk I trench knife. This had a 6¾in. double-edged blade and a brass-knuckle grip. The M1942 machete had an 18in. blade and proved to be a valuable tool.

Every man in a rifle company was expected to have at least a rudimentary ability to operate every weapon. All men were also trained to operate basic Japanese weapons.

Web gear

The "TA 50 gear" (Table of Allowance), or "web gear," used by paratroopers was little different from that used by the standard infantry. However, there were some specialized items used by paratroopers – mainly jump containers. Before late 1943, web gear was OD shade no. 9, a tan or very light brown shade. Dark brownish green OD shade no. 7, which began being issued in early 1944, provided better camouflage, especially in the jungle. Shade no. 9 gear remained in use throughout the war and might have been mixed with shade no. 7 items.

Parachute infantrymen carried an M1910 canteen carrier with a 1qt canteen and canteen cup; an M1924 or M1942 first aid kit; an M1910 T-handle or M1943 folding entrenching tool and carrier; and an M1936 field bag, better known as a "musette bag." Paratroopers were issued this pouch-like bag, which was carried by a shoulder strap, instead of the awkward M1928 haversack used by other infantrymen. It could also be carried on the back attached to the M1936 suspenders. The musette bag proved to be too small for jungle operations where units did not always receive timely resupply. The larger jungle pack began to be issued in late 1943. It had integral shoulder straps with a large cargo compartment and a smaller compartment on the top flap. Some troops cut the top flap compartment off and used it as a haversack. The foregoing items were attached to a web belt depending on the soldier's weapon.

Men armed with the M1 or M1903 rifle were issued the M1923 dismounted cartridge belt. It had ten pockets each holding an eight-round clip for the M1 or two five-round loading clips for the M1903 (80 and 100 rounds, respectively). Those armed with the M1A1 carbine and submachine guns had an M1936 pistol belt. Those with carbines had at least two magazine pouches, each holding two 15-round magazines. The carbine pouch was redesigned in 1944 and the magazine pockets could now hold M1 rifle clips as an alternative means of carrying ammunition. Some riflemen carried up to six of these, each holding two clips, on a pistol belt. Ammunition for Thompsons that used 20-round magazines was carried in a pouch holding five magazines and those soldiers with Thompsons and grease guns with 30-round magazines had a three-magazine pouch. Men armed with the BAR carried an M1937 magazine belt. It had six pockets, each holding two 20-round magazines. Owing to weight, it was recommended that eight magazines be carried in four pockets and the other two pockets be used for cleaning gear. Men armed with a pistol had an M1918 or

Assorted equipment is unpacked from an aerial equipment container. The equipment includes: a barber's clipper, scissors and comb; two DR-5 telephone wire reels; .30-cal machine gun belts; two TS-10 sound-powered telephones; and an SCR-511 "pogo-stick" radio. (Tom Laemlein, Armor Plate Press)

M1923 magazine pouch for two seven-round magazines. Some units were issued M1923 mounted cartridge belts, which lacked the left front clip pocket that allowed the pistol magazine pouch to be attached. Some troops simply cut the left front clip pocket off a dismounted belt so that they could attach a pistol magazine pouch. Many eased the burden of their web gear with the M1936 belt suspenders. The ammunition carrying bag, or "general purpose

Paratroopers' individual equipment, 503rd PIR, 1943

This example of a parachutist rifleman's equipment demonstrates the equipment used by the 503rd PIR. The equipment varied over time and between units. All items were carried on his belt or in his pockets.

M1C steel helmet, liner, parachutist's chinstrap
T-5 troop parachute assembly, main and reserve
Type B-4 inflatable life vest (worn under parachute harness if overflying water)
Herringbone fatigue uniform, M1937 waist belt
Parachutist's boots (Corcorans)
Leather gloves
Mosquito head net
Undershirt, under drawers, socks, identification tags
Poncho
M1936 musette bag
Four Mk II fragmentation hand grenades (some carried two frags and two M15 WP)
.45-cal M1911A1 pistol, M1 holster
M1923 pistol magazine pouch, two seven-round magazines
30ft parachutist's lowering rope
Six D-ration bars
.30-cal M1 rifle, M1907 leather sling
M1905 bayonet
M1918 Mk I trench knife (brass-knuckle grip)
M1942 machete
M1936 pistol belt, five clip pouches for 200 rounds .30-cal, M1936 suspenders
M1910 1qt canteen, cup, carrier (later two were carried)
M1942 first aid pouch, field dressing, sulfanilamide (sulfa anti-infection) powder packet, morphine syrette
Large field dressing, mosquito repellent, foot powder
Halazone water purification tablets, atabrine anti-malaria tablets, salt tablets
Map, message book, two pencils
M2 switchblade pocket knife, pocket compass, match container
Rifle oil, bore cleaner, cleaning patches
M1926 spoon

ammo bag," was issued on the basis of two per man, although it was not widely used. It could carry hand and rifle grenades, submachine gun magazines, rifle ammunition bandoliers, or machine gun belts. M1 rifle ammunition was issued in six-pocket bandoliers, one eight-round clip per pocket. Paratroopers often entered combat with one or two bandoliers.

M3-series gas masks were issued, but were seldom carried into combat in the Pacific.

The T-5 troop parachute

The T-5 troop type parachute was introduced in 1942 replacing the T-4, a modified aviator's emergency parachute with the addition of a reserve. The T-5's three-point release harness consisted of a web seat and torso harness with snaphook fastened leg and chest straps that hooked to D-rings. The 5,000lb test white cotton webbing straps passed around the torso, formed a seat, looped between the legs, and ran back up to the shoulders to terminate in four 3ft-long riser straps. The canopy suspension lines were attached to connector links at the end of the risers. The harness also possessed a belly band to which the reserve was attached along with a pair of D-rings on the harness front. The pack tray contained the canopy, stowed suspension lines, and the ends of the risers that were attached to the harnesses' back. The main canopy was 28ft in diameter and constructed of 28 long, narrow pie-shaped panels. At the canopy's apex was an 18in. diameter hole which allowed air to be vented. This helped reduce oscillation (swinging from side to side). Although there appeared to be 28 individual suspension lines, there were actually 14. These ran from a connector link on the riser attached to the harness, through a canopy seam, over the canopy's apex and then down another seam to be connected to a connector link on a riser on the other side of the harness. Seven lines were attached to each connector link on the end of the risers. From riser to canopy skirt the exposed suspension lines were 22ft long. The nylon canopies were three-color camouflage patterned – tannish light green base with dark and medium green splotches. From a distance they appeared to be solid OD. The reserve parachute was 22ft in diameter (T-5A was 24ft), packed in a chest-mounted container, and opened by a ripcord handle on the container's right end. There were two snaphooks, fastened to the reserve canopy's short risers, on the reserve container's back that attached to the main harnesses' D-rings. Reserve canopies were white. The main and reserve containers were made of OD cotton canvas. Attached to the pack tray cover was a 15ft white static line with a heavy fastener hook that attached to the jump aircraft's anchor line cable. The reason canopies were camouflaged was to make it difficult for enemy fighters to locate recently used drop zones and attack assembling troops. They were also used by paratroopers to camouflage weapon positions, command posts, supply dumps, and even vehicles.

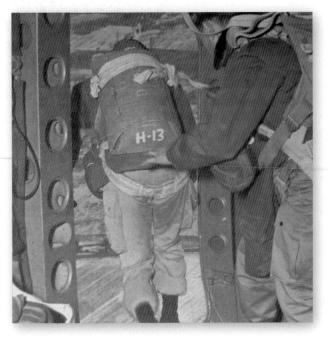

A paratrooper makes a vigorous exit from a C-47 transport. This demonstrates how the static line was secured to the back of the main parachute backpack and also how the parachute harness formed a seat to support the jumper. (US Army)

BELIEF AND BELONGING

Paratroopers were renowned for their *esprit de corps*. This was developed throughout the Parachute Course. Jump school was one of the few courses during which both officers and enlisted men undertook exactly the same training and harassment together. That experience created a unique and strong bond through the ranks. Of course, officers were free after hours while the enlisted were restricted to company areas, but that made little difference. The only difference between an NCO instructor dropping a captain and a private for push-ups was the former was granted the courtesy of, "Give me twenty-five, Sir!" There was more to it than simply undertaking the training side by side. The men saw their leaders enduring the same physical exertion, punishments, and risks as themselves and saw how they performed as leaders leading runs and checking on their men. The officers saw first hand how their men handled the ordeal.

Jumping out of airplanes had another effect on morale. No matter how realistic and grueling combat training was, no matter how miserable the weather and terrain might be, it was still training with safety constraints. There were training accidents, vehicle mishaps, and accidental shootings, but a parachute descent, or more accurately, the landing (only the last quarter-inch hurts), could result in fractures, back and muscle injuries, and abrasions. There were also hazards from landing in trees, on power lines, in bodies of water, and on obstacles – from boulders to vehicles to buildings. Parachute malfunctions, while not frequent, did occur and reserve parachutes did not always save the day if deployed too low, or if they did not fully inflate, or they became tangled. There were indeed fatalities, occasionally one or two during a regimental jump. That does not mean that paratroopers were braver than other troops. However, the inherent danger they faced and knowingly having placed themselves in a potentially dangerous situation, as opposed to simply confronting a deadly situation when it arose, prepared them to deal with stress and control fear.

In many cases, the parachute units assigned to a particular division had been raised earlier and begun training, often in a different location. By the time they joined their division they were an organized unit with their own *esprit de corps*. The paratroopers, who made up only a quarter of the division's strength, considered themselves superior to their straight-leg counterparts and they made no secret of this fact. Fights in service clubs and off-post bars were common.

Officially, the 11th was nicknamed the "Angels," but the troops were soon calling themselves "Hell's Angels", in a further show of cockiness.

Paratroopers had a great deal of loyalty to their units. Many, unless they had been selected as cadre for a new unit, served their entire WWII career in the same unit from the day it was activated. There were several regiments that never left the States or

This paratrooper has his M1A1 carbine stowed behind his reserve parachute. Folded under the reserve is a Type AN 6505-1 aviator's kit bag. This was carried during training jumps and the opened main parachute, backpack, and harness were figure-eight rolled and stuffed into the bag. The reserve was then clipped to its carrying handles, and the whole thing was carried to the turn-in point before the follow-on tactical exercise was conducted. (Tom Laemlein, Armor Plate Press)

deployed late in the war and their troops were often assigned as replacements for divisional regiments.

A wounded paratrooper, unless sent out of theater for treatment, was typically reassigned to his original company, but seldom to the same platoon or squad owing to replacements having been assigned in his absence.

Organization

The parachute infantry regiment had three 530-man battalions, each with a 149-man headquarters company and three 127-man rifle companies. The company's three rifle platoons were organized much differently from the standard platoons. Rather than having a single platoon commander, the parachute platoon had two officers. Two C-47s were required to airlift a platoon and one officer would be assigned to each aircraft. It was felt that two officers could more quickly assemble the scattered, air-dropped platoon. One officer could lead the bulk of the assembled platoon on to the objective, while the other remained at the assembly point to collect stragglers. Of course, two officers meant there could be a quick replacement if one became a casualty. In reality, the second officer was not always assigned. If he was, then he served more as an understudy and provided immediately available replacements for other platoons if necessary.

The platoon's radio and code corporal (sometimes called the "radio and wire corporal") and radio operator were also unique to the airborne units. It was originally envisioned that parachute platoons might conduct semi-independent raids. They were to be equipped with a longer-range radio and code encryption device. This equipment was never issued.

The platoon headquarters received a bazooka in early 1944. These were often manned by ad hoc 2–3-man teams. Rather than three rifle squads the parachute platoon had only two. Since the BAR had to be dropped in a separate parachute container, the squad was given more firepower in the form of a Browning light machine gun. This was less mobile than a BAR, though, and required a three-man crew. On paper, squads also had a second Browning that would be dropped later or brought in by the ground echelon for use in

E **LIGHT MACHINE GUN TEAM, MANILA, FEBRUARY 1945**

Each of a parachute rifle company's six rifle squads had a .30-cal Browning M1919A4 light machine gun. Many squads replaced it with a .30-cal M1918A2 BAR for a more maneuverable weapon in the jungle and hills. The squad LMG crew consisted of a machine gunner, assistant gunner, and ammunition bearer. There was also a second spare gun, which saw little use. The battalion headquarters company was assigned a light machine gun platoon, the tactical equivalent of the two heavy machine gun platoons found in the standard infantry battalion weapons company. However, they lacked the range, accuracy, and sustained rate of fire of the Browning M1917A1 water-cooled machine gun used by the heavy machine gunners. The platoon had a five-man HQ (platoon commander, platoon sergeant, instrument corporal, two messengers) and two sections, each with a staff sergeant and four five-man squads. The squads had a sergeant squad leader, machine gunner, assistant gunner, and two ammunition bearers. The 503rd PIR's battalions formed three four-squad machine gun platoons, one for attachment to each rifle company since they were mostly armed with BARs. They deleted the sections and used four-man crews. Web-belted ammunition was packed in 250-round cans. Here the belts are loaded with four armor-piercing (black tip) and one tracer (red tip) rounds, the AP rounds providing better penetration through cover materials. The platoon commander is using an SCR-536 "handie-talkie" AM radio fitted with a rigger-made jump harness allowing it to be attached to the parachute harness. An M9 hand pyrotechnic projector for firing 37mm double-star signal flares sits ready beside him. This 511th PIR gun crew is engaged in the penetration of the fortified Genko Line on the south side of Manila. The vicious fight lasted from February 4 until February 24.

A platoon radio operator's equipment laid out on a shelter half. Top to bottom, left to right: T-5 troop parachute, AL-140 air-to-ground signal panels and pins, T-5 reserve parachute, .30-cal M1 rifle, Griswold weapons container, M1905 bayonet, SCR-536 "handie-talkie" radio with parachute jump harness, mosquito head net, gloves, 33ft parachute rope, two 30-round submachine gun magazine cases each with three signal flares for the 37mm M4 ground signal projector (carried by the platoon leader), M1936 pistol belt with M1936 suspenders, M1918 pistol magazine pouch, five rigger-made M1 rifle clip pouches (five clips each – 200 rounds), M1942 18in. machete, M1910 canteen and carrier, M1942 first aid pouch, M1 holster with .45-cal M1911A1 pistol, and M1918 Mk I trench knife. M2 artillery compass, TL-122A flashlight, notepad and M-210 message book, pencils, M2 pocketknife, five small field dressings, bandage, foot powder, three assorted pill bottles, toothbrush, M1926 spoon, and four Mk II fragmentation grenades (bottom grenade is pre-1943 yellow-painted). (Tom Laemlein, Armor Plate Press)

Parachute rifle platoon, 1942–44 (according to T/O&E)

Platoon Headquarters	7 soldiers	37 soldiers in total in a platoon
Platoon Commander	1st lieutenant	M1A1 carbine
Asst Platoon Commander	2nd lieutenant	M1A1 carbine
Platoon Sergeant	staff sergeant	M1928A1 SMG
Radio and Code Corporal	corporal	M1 rifle
Radio Operator	pvt/pfc	M1 rifle
Messenger (x2)	pvt/pfc	M1 rifle
2.36in. M1A1 bazooka		
Rifle Squad (x2)	12 soldiers	
Squad Leader	sergeant	M1 rifle
Asst Squad Leader[1]	corporal	M1928A1 SMG
Light Machine Gunner	pvt/pfc	M1919A4 LMG, M1911A1 pistol
Asst Light Machine Gunner	pvt/pfc	M1 rifle
Ammunition Bearer	pvt/pfc	M1 rifle
Rifleman (x7)	pvt/pfc	M1 rifle
M1919A4 LMG (x2)[2]		
M7 grenade launcher (x2)[3]		
Mortar Squad	6 soldiers	
Squad Leader	sergeant	M1928A1 SMG
Mortar Gunner	pvt/pfc	M2 mortar, M1 rifle
Asst Mortar Gunner	pvt/pfc	M1 rifle
Ammunition Bearer (x3)	pvt/pfc	M1 rifle
Total weapons		
M1 rifle	29	
M1A1 carbine	2	
M1928A1 SMG	4	
M1911A1 pistol[4]	37	
M1919A4 LMG	4	
60mm M2 mortar	1	
2.36in M1A1 bazooka[5]	1	
M7 grenade launcher	4	
SCR-536 "handie-talkie" radio	1 (On company command net)	

1 The assistant squad leader was assigned additional duty as demolition NCO.
2 One LMG assigned, dedicated crew (often replaced by BAR), one additional unmanned LMG for optional use.
3 M7 grenade launchers carried by two riflemen.
4 One per man, but often not issued/carried. Withdrawn from issue in February 1944.
5 An unmanned bazooka was authorized for platoon HQ in February 1944.

the defense. It would be manned by the assistant machine gunner and a riflemen. Often in the 503rd and 511th light machine guns were replaced by BARs to improve mobility and ease of use in the jungle. Some squads retained both to give them more options. The assistant squad leader doubled as the demolition NCO responsible for training the rest of the squad and supervising demolition work. This was again a holdover from the raider concept. On paper, two riflemen were designated scouts, but this was often ignored as all squad members were considered scouts. One or two riflemen would be assigned as grenadiers. After only a short time in combat it was common for rifle squads to number between six and nine men.

Company officers of the 503rd on New Guinea study a map. The officer to the left is armed with a Thompson M1928A1 submachine gun. Note the M1942 machete and M17 binocular case on the officer to the right. (Tom Laemlein, Armor Plate Press)

The third squad manned the 60mm mortar providing immediate line-of-sight fire support. Standard rifle companies had a weapons platoon with three 60mm mortars and two light machine guns. The parachute company lacked such a platoon. In some instances companies formed an ad hoc mortar platoon to concentrate their fire. In other cases between two and four men would be added to the mortar squad to allow it to be used as a third rifle squad. It could employ its mortar if necessary, but in dense jungles the use of mortars was restricted or impossible. The 503rd adopted a three-rifle squad organization before Nadzab, two with BARs and the third with a machine gun. The three 60mm squads were formed into a company mortar platoon.

The rifle company headquarters was composed of a captain CO, 1st lieutenant XO, 1st sergeant, communication and operations sergeants, three radio operators, three messengers, and five riflemen. The latter were supposed to serve as immediate replacements. However, in reality they were assigned to squads.

The parachute rifle company lacked supply personnel, clerks, and other service troops normally assigned to the headquarters. Instead, services were centralized. Mess personnel were in the battalion headquarters company. Other service personnel were in the 208-man regimental service company responsible for administration, supply, and motor maintenance. The service company possessed all of the regiment's motor vehicles (one sedan, 13 jeeps, two ambulances, eight ¾-ton command trucks, 16 2½-ton cargo trucks, 14 1-ton trailers). The battalion headquarters company consisted of the headquarters, mortar (four 81mm M1s), and light machine gun (eight .30-cal M1919A4s) platoons. The 503rd PIR formed three four-gun light machine gun platoons with one attached to each rifle company.

The 160-man regimental headquarters and headquarters company had communication and demolition (with a section for attachment to each battalion, which was sometimes used for reconnaissance) platoons, as well as operations and intelligence staff sections. There was also a 69-man medical detachment operating regimental and battalion aid stations and providing medics to platoons.

The 503rd and 511th PIRs were assigned parachute artillery battalions (457th and 462nd, respectively). They had a headquarters and service battery, medical detachment, three firing batteries with four 75mm M1A1 pack howitzers each, and an antiaircraft/antitank battery. The 457th rearmed its

A battery of 75mm M1A1 howitzers on M3A2 carriages of the 675th Glider Field Artillery Battalion in the Nichols Field area south on Manila, February 1945. All three of the 11th Abn Div's field artillery battalions (457th Parachute, 674th and 675th Glider) and the 503rd PRCT's 462nd Parachute were armed with the "pack 75." In mid-January 1945, the 457th PFAB had been rearmed with 105mm M3 howitzers. (Tom Laemlein, Armor Plate Press)

Battery D with 75mm howitzers and the 462nd with 12 .50-cal M2 machine guns replacing the four 37mm AT guns.

Awards and decorations

Individual and unit awards for valor, achievement, and service were valuable for recognizing soldierly qualities and for morale and motivation.

The Bronze Star Medal was not authorized until February 1944, but made retroactive to December 7, 1941. It was the lowest valor award, rating below the Silver Star Medal, Distinguished Service Cross, and Medal of Honor. Large numbers of Bronze Stars were presented. Subsequent awards were denoted by small bronze oak leaf clusters. From 1947 soldiers awarded the Combat Infantryman's Badge (CIB) could apply for the Bronze Star for combat service because the CIB was awarded "only to soldiers who had borne combat duties befitting the recognition conferred by a Bronze Star." The Purple Heart was awarded for wounds received in combat as a result of enemy action. It was also bestowed on those killed in action.

Sergeant Ray E. Eubanks of Company D, 503rd, was posthumously awarded the Medal of Honor for action on Noemfoor Island. The 511th had two Medal of Honor recipients, both posthumous: Pvt Elmer E. Fryar of Company E on Leyte and Pfc Manuel Perez, Jr. of Company A during the assault on Ft William McKinley on Luzon. Additionally, members of the

Aircrews of the 317th Troop Carrier Group are briefed planeside at the Lipa Airfield on Luzon in preparation for the Camalaniugan jump by the 11th Abn Div's Gypsy Task Force, which was built around 1/511th PIR by attaching reinforcing units. This was the last combat jump of World War II. (Tom Laemlein, Armor Plate Press)

511th were presented four Distinguished Service Crosses, 140 Silver Stars, 12 Soldier's Medals, 25 Air Medals, and scores of Bronze Stars. (No comparable list has been found for the 503rd.)

The 503rd earned Campaign Streamers inscribed with New Guinea, Leyte, Luzon (with Assault Arrowhead), and Southern Philippines. The unit also received the Presidential Unit Citation for Corregidor. The 511th's Campaign Streamers are inscribed with New Guinea, Leyte, and Luzon (with Assault Arrowhead). It also earned Presidential Unit Citations for Manila and Luzon. Both units received the Philippine Presidential Unit Citation for the period from October 17, 1944, to July 4, 1945. The Philippine awards were bestowed in 1950. The award of the Campaign Streamers, at the end of the war, paralleled the award of the Asiatic-Pacific Campaign Medal to all personnel participating in operations in the Pacific – a small bronze Campaign Star ("battle star") was attached to the ribbon for each named campaign the recipient participated in. The World War II Victory Medal was presented to all servicemen and women serving between December 7, 1941, and December 31, 1946. Members of the 511th on occupation duty in Japan were granted the Army of Occupation Medal for 30 consecutive days' occupation duty between September 1945 and April 1952. All personnel serving in the Philippines were authorized the Philippine Liberation Medal for 30 consecutive days in the archipelago between October 7, 1944, and September 2, 1945. This was a Philippine Government award.

Parachute infantrymen who saw combat were awarded the Combat Infantryman's Badge, one of the Army's most coveted decorations. The CIB was approved in November 1943 and made retroactive to December 7, 1941. There was no prescribed duration in combat the criteria being that: "The Soldier must be an Infantryman satisfactorily performing Infantry duties, must be assigned to an Infantry unit during such time as the unit is engaged in active ground combat, and must actively participate in such ground combat." The CIB was composed of a silver-edged infantry blue bar with a silver musket and wreath. At the time, the CIB was typically worn above the left breast pocket and below any ribbons, while the jumpwings were worn above the ribbons. Enlisted men awarded the CIB (but not officers) received an additional $10 a month.

CONDITIONS OF SERVICE

Paratroopers were like any other troops, in that they needed to be kept occupied. This was accomplished by extensive and demanding training, endless work details, make-work details, and various diversions, both on and off post. The Army provided extensive on-post diversions in the form of libraries; gymnasiums; athletic fields; bowling allies; enlisted, NCO (corporals up) and officer clubs; movie theaters; playhouses; and other activities. Units often organized intramural sports with unit teams, the most popular being softball and basketball. It was preferred to keep troops on-post as nearby towns were typically awash with bars, pool halls, illegal gambling, and prostitution. There were all sorts of scams to separate often naive GIs from their money. There were also United Service Organization shows and dances in local USO halls and on-post. Local towns also organized dances and social events for the troops. There were other areas that played a major part in the life of a soldier as the following pages will show.

Troops in transit crossing the country in troop trains are given free sandwiches and coffee by community volunteers as they pass through a small town railroad station. (National Archives)

Troop trains

Unit long-distance moves were conducted by troop trains. US railroads moved 44 million service personnel during the war. Regular passenger cars, Pullman sleepers, and club cars were used, as were Army-built 50ft troop sleepers, kitchen cars, and hospital cars. Troop train travel was boring and rarely comfortable. While regular Pullman sleepers and troop sleepers were supposed to be used for trips of over 12 hours, they were not always available and troops often had to sleep in their seats or in aisles. Technically, the Army could divert Pullmans from civilian trains on less than 450-mile runs. When Pullmans and troop sleepers were available, there would be a civilian porter in each car and bedding and linen would be changed daily, as was the case during civilian use. A troop sleeper accommodated 39 men and the porter. In daytime, the bunks were folded up and the seats lowered. There were weapons racks, four washstands, two toilets, and a water cooler. The more exclusive Pullmans were generally reserved for officers. Troop kitchen cars were operated by Army cooks with embarked troops pulling KP. There were two coal cooking ranges, a 200-gal water tank, a water heater, a refrigerator, storage, and food preparation areas. These cars were placed in the middle of the train and chow was served in mess kits from both ends to serve 250 men, who ate in their passenger cars. When club and dining cars were available they were operated by civilians and meals were served on china and tablecloths. Mostly, these were reserved for officers.

Long-distance train travel was tiring as sleep was often interrupted. There were few, if any, opportunities to bath or even shave, and troops generally wore the same uniform for the entire trip. Card games, gambling, reading, and "jawing" were the main diversions. Meals were often light and there were many complaints that there was not enough to go around. Troops hanging out of windows would give civilians money at stations to buy food, snacks, or more commonly, beer and liquor. Soldiers were sometimes disconcerted when the train pulled out before the civilians returned. Some civilians walked off with the money with no intention of making purchases. Soldiers often were not allowed off trains during stops in order to reduce AWOLs, or simply because of the fear that they might not reboard in time. Sometimes, they were allowed off to visit free canteens providing refreshments. Many towns organized volunteer and church groups which provided free home-cooked meals or snacks. "Platform girls" bearing baskets of sandwiches and snacks handed the free goodies to soldiers hanging out of windows. There were sometimes rest stops when troops un-boarded and exercised or even stripped to underwear and washed under the train's water tower.

When trains rolled in to their destination the troops were more than ready for the trip to end, even if it meant that they had arrived at an overseas replacement depot and were bound for their port of embarkation.

Camp Stoneman

Camp Stoneman was the main West Coast replacement depot and staging base. It was at Pittsburg, California, 40 miles northeast of San Francisco with its

Port of Embarkation. Over a million troops bound for the Pacific staged through Camp Stoneman, which had accommodations for 38,000 troops in two-story wooden barracks. The 511th spent 16 days there from April 23 to May 8, 1944. The replacement depot received, processed, housed, and fed a continuous flow of units arriving by train from all over the country. All personnel were given medical and dental examinations and corrective dental work was undertaken. They stood in long lines for seemingly endless inoculations for diseases they had never heard of. Personal and financial records were brought up to date along with wills, GI insurance, and next-of-kin notifications. As the information entered on dog tags frequently changed, deploying troops often received new ones. "Showdown inspections" ensured all clothing and equipment were in order, any shortages were made up, and worn items were replaced. In some cases, entire units were issued with tropical clothing as they arrived from colder climates and all training-worn equipment was replaced with the latest issue. Units were afforded time to conduct some final training, which might include first aid, shipboard procedures and duties, field sanitation, tropical diseases and hazards, physical exercises and runs, and zeroing their weapons on the range. Vehicles on flatcars and unit equipment in boxcars were taken directly to the port of embarkation to load aboard transports.

Roll call was taken twice daily. Troops were restricted to post, but ample entertainment was provided for diversion and to keep morale up, including three movie theaters, a 10,000-seat outdoor theater, eight post exchanges, gymnasiums, baseball fields, and a huge service club with weekly USO shows. Many entertainers came up from Hollywood and performed there. When the departure day came, units were moved to the San Francisco Port of Embarkation either by the Army-operated former excursion boats *Catalina* and *Cabrillo* and the million-dollar ferry *Yerba Buena* or, occasionally, by truck convoy. Final letters were written to parents, wives, and sweethearts. Long lines formed at the banks of phone booths and post chapels were filled.

Camp Stoneman, CA, the main West Coast replacement depot and staging base. Both the 503rd and 511th PIRs passed through the camp en route to the Pacific. The two-story barracks were among the better accommodations that the regiments had experienced. (US Army)

Embarked

Embarkation orders were typed listing every man assigned to the unit. Soldiers were frequently reminded that missing a troop movement was a court martial offense. There was a final inspection that ensured they had everything they needed. At the ship's gangplank each man was checked off the roster as he struggled up the ramp with his helmet, web gear, gas mask, weapons, and duffel bag. Few troops had ever been aboard any kind of ship. A sailor led each group into the bowels down endless companionways and ladders.

The troop quarters were cramped and poorly ventilated. There were few portholes, none for those near, or below, the waterline. Portholes had to be closed at night and in rough weather. Forced air ventilation was inadequate. Troop bunks or "racks" were pipe frames with 2ft x 6ft canvas "mattresses" rope-laced to them. Stacked between three and six high, there was only 18–24in. clearance between them. Aisles between racks were only wide enough for a man to squeeze through. Duffle bags and gear were stowed under bottom bunks. As there was not enough room for everything, the excess was simply stacked in the aisles and had to be climbed over. Below decks it was hot, often damp, stuffy, and smelled of sweat and, once they had departed, vomit. The heads (latrines) and washrooms smelled worse even though they were swabbed daily.

Once out of port, the troops were free to explore the ship and go on deck. There were, of course, restricted areas and outsiders were not generally welcomed into unit areas unescorted. Friends from different units would meet on deck. So many troops were on deck that space was at a premium. Lifejackets were required on deck, no lights or smoking were allowed at night, and nothing could be thrown overboard. Smoking was allowed only when the public address system announced, "The smoking lamp is lit." There were lifeboat, fire, and air raid drills. The troops quickly fell into shipboard routine. The worst part for many was seasickness and this was extremely debilitating to the point where victims felt that they would welcome death. The sickness might last for three days or so. If bad weather were encountered, it could reoccur. In the close conditions, sanitation was poor. Saltwater showers dried the skin and no one felt clean after using rock-hard saltwater soap. Ships absorbed heat during the day so at night it was sweltering below decks owing to the trapped heat and poor ventilation. Many troops opted to sleep on deck.

Shipboard life, once the novelty wore off, was monotonous. Card and dice games were unending. Some played more mundane board games, read, or wrote letters, which would be censored by officers before they could be sent. The ship's crew usually mimeographed a newsletter which contained news gleaned from shortwave radio broadcasts. Reveille and other calls were blared over the never silent PA. There were only two meals a day for which the men stood in line for two hours, eventually receiving poor to moderate food ladled into trays. They stood at long, chest-high tables, moving along the table while eating. At the end of the table they washed their trays. There were occasional classes and sometimes calisthenics. Weapons were sometimes test-fired off the stern. The officers always seemed to be having meetings and briefings.

The 511th was aboard ship for 22 days, for the period of May 8–29, 1944, en route to New Guinea. As they arrived, the troops lined the railing to catch a view of their destination. They were soon ordered below deck to load up and prepare for debarkation.

First aid

The hot, wet, humid tropical environment in which the paratroopers operated was a breeding ground for disease and illnesses. Malaria, dysentery, yaws, filariasis, elephantiasis, blackwater fever, dengue fever, hepatitis, leprosy, and hookworms and other parasites were common. The ghastly living conditions in a combat environment only enhanced the combatants' suffering. High temperatures, humidity, rain, swamps, mud, broken terrain, physical exhaustion, sleep deprivation, insufficient and irregular diet, dehydration, and mental stress resulted in a high incidence of combat fatigue, accidents, self-inflicted wounds, tropical ulcers, immersion foot, diarrhea, rashes, and unidentified fevers. Unburied bodies and infestations of disease-carrying flies aggravated the unsanitary conditions. There were also poisonous snakes and spiders, centipedes, fleas, lice, mosquitoes, and ants to contend with.

US medical support was well organized and effective. Despite this, the awful conditions made it essential for individual paratroopers to care for themselves to the greatest extent possible. Even minor scratches could very rapidly become severely infected or turn into tropical ulcers – lesions, usually on the legs, which eroded muscles and tendons.

Not only were first aid items carried, but also sanitation and health preservation items. Each paratrooper carried an M1942 first aid pouch with a Carlisle small (4 × 7in.) field dressing, sulfanilamide powder packet, and a morphine syrette. The latter was not normally carried by infantrymen but, as paratroopers were more likely to be separated from their platoon, they were supplied with one. In their musette bag, or pockets, they might carry one or more additional field dressings, a single large (7½ × 8in.) field dressing, insect repellent, foot powder, and a variety of pills: halazone water purification, atabrine anti-malaria, and salt tablets. Additional field dressings were carried owing to the probablity of entry and exit wounds and multiple fragmentation wounds. From 1944, many carried an M2 jungle first aid kit with athlete's foot solution, iodine, insect repellent, eight sulfa tablets, water purification tablets, three adhesive compresses, field dressing, and 30 atabrine anti-malaria tablets. It was common to modify the contents to one's own preference. (The parachute first aid kit so widely used in Europe – tied to the helmet netting –

Nadzab, Northeast New Guinea, September 5, 1943. The 503rd PIR jumps from C-47s at 500ft to secure the airfield and block a Japanese withdrawal as Australian forces attack overland and from the sea in a pincer movement. The flanking smoke screen was laid by A-20 attack aircraft. This was the first US airborne operation in the Pacific and the only one in which an entire regiment was dropped on the same day. (Tom Laemlein, Armor Plate Press)

was little used in the Pacific. It contained a field dressing, tourniquet, and morphine syrette.)

Sulfanilamide ("sulfa") powder (introduced in late 1941) and tablets (introduced in early 1942) were useful for preventing infection. Crystalline sulfa powder was provided in a five-gram paper packet that was to be sprinkled evenly on the wound before applying the dressing. It was often packed inside the field dressing. A packet of eight sulfa tablets was also issued. Unless wounded in the throat or abdomen (it could induce nausea and abdominal cramps), soldiers were to take all eight tablets with at least a half-canteen of water. They were told not to take the tablets unless there was sufficient water or wine as it could crystallize and the kidneys would not absorb it properly. By mid-1944 it was determined that sulfa powder was ineffective. It allowed the introduction of foreign particles and, since it could not reach deep into the wound, was of little value. The much more effective penicillin was coming into wider use instead.

The Army adopted the ½-grain morphine syrette in 1940 as the primary means of injecting the potent painkiller. Newsreel reports often touted how brave wounded troops silently suffered their wounds. That was because they were dosed with morphine. It was injected into the abdomen, thigh, or upper arm. Full effects were not felt for between 20–30 minutes. It was not to be administered for pain in the abdomen, unconsciousness, head injuries, reduced respiration (under 12 breaths per minute), within two hours of an earlier dose, or before impending surgery in which general anesthetic would be used. Medics pinned the used syrette through the soldier's collar, marked an "M" on the forehead, and indicated the time administered on the casualty tag. This prevented double-dosing at aid stations.

An aidman, or medic, was attached to each rifle platoon from the battalion section of the regimental medical detachment. Medics, almost universally called "Doc," undertook 13 weeks of basic training to learn common soldier skills, fieldcraft, and combat medical training. Their medical aid bags contained only minimal items: dressings, bandages, and basic medications. They mainly tried to stop bleeding, prevent shock, and keep the wounded breathing until they could be evacuated to the battalion aid station. They spent much of their effort taking care of simple aches and pains and minor injuries and illnesses within their platoon.

A paratrooper undergoing unit training eats a K-ration meal. He is armed with an M1A1 carbine. His web gear includes the M1936 pistol belt with two-pocket carbine magazine pouches, M1936 suspenders, and an M1910 entrenching tool. (Tom Laemlein, Armor Plate Press)

K-rats

Field rations Type K were introduced in 1942 as assault rations for no more than 15 consecutive meals. However, it was not uncommon for troops to subsist on "Ks" for weeks, and even months. Besides being repetitive, they were deficient in vitamins, calories, and bulk, leaving men hungry. K-rations, a "ration" being three meals, were issued in three pocket-size cartons designated breakfast, dinner, and supper, although troops ate what was available or what they preferred. The K rations were as follows:

Breakfast: canned chopped ham and eggs or veal loaf, crackers, dried fruit or cereal bar, water-purification tablets, four cigarettes, chewing gum, instant coffee, and sugar.

Dinner: canned cheese spread, ham, or ham and cheese, crackers, malted milk tablets or caramels, sugar, salt, cigarettes, book of matches, chewing gum, and a powdered beverage packet (lemon, orange, grape).

Supper: canned chicken paté, sausage, pork luncheon meat with carrot and apple or beef and pork, crackers, chocolate bar, toilet paper, cigarettes, chewing gum, and bouillon soup cube or powder.

D-ration chocolate bars were issued for emergencies. The special mixture would not soften below 120°F. The "Logan bar" was specified to "taste little better than boiled potato" to prevent soldiers from snacking on it. Paratroopers jumped in with between three and six of the thick, 4oz, enriched chocolate bars and usually three K-rat meals. Deane E. Marks[6] of 2/511th describes the ritual of eating a K-rat on Leyte:

Morning finally came, so we dug out our Ks and started thinking about breakfast. The best way to heat water for coffee (Nescafe Powder) was to start the fire with the heavily waxed cardboard box that the K-ration came in. These boxes burned well. The mosquito repellent was also flammable and could be used to get a good hot fire going. Dry twigs were hard to come by, but once the K-ration box was going good, small twigs would start to burn. Once you had the fire going, you could increase the diameter size of the twigs and soon have a good sized fire. I used to get a canteen cup of water boiling, pop an envelope of bullion [sic] powder in and then put all the saltine crackers into the boiling bullion [sic], along with whatever meat I had. Sometimes it was chopped pork with egg yolk added, other times it was spam. The meat came in an OD colored can about the size of a tuna can seen today. It was good and had plenty of nutrition and would stick to your ribs. For desert, the Ks contained a fruit bar (dried raisins, apricots, pressed together in a bar about ¾in square and 3in long) to munch on. Another menu had a Hershey Tropical Chocolate D [-ration] bar. A solid chocolate (hard as a rock) lump which you could chomp on or could melt it in boiling water and you'd end up with a cup of rather flat cocoa. There were also six little rock hard candy wafers, about ¾in square × ³⁄₁₆in thick that you could suck on. Half of these were plain dextrose pills and the other three were chocolate flavored. They gave instant energy, as they were pure sugar. Also, in one of the menus was a little tuna can of American processed cheese. Dub Westbrook loved this stuff and always toasted it on the end of his GI fork. The cheese menu also had an envelope of grape powder or lemonade mix. I remember these well as they were made by "Miles Laboratories" who brings us Alka-Seltzer. You topped all this off with a stick of Wrigley's gum in an OD wrapper, as you sat back and enjoyed your Luckies or Camels, which were also included. There were only four cigs in a box, like the ones we used to get on the airliners. I didn't smoke, so mine were up for grabs. Also included, was a little packet of OD colored toilet paper, which you would tuck into your breast pocket for later use.

6 All Deane E. Marks excerpts are from his article, "No One Smiled on Leyte," in *Winds Aloft* newsletter of the 511th PIR Association.

ON CAMPAIGN

Two operations will be described to give an example of campaign experience. The 511th's first major combat jump was onto Tagaytay Ridge on Luzon, on November 3–4, 1944. It was a less than spectacular operation with the troops experiencing the problems typical of large airborne operations. It achieved its goal and placed an entire regiment in position to pursue the withdrawing Japanese without the troops having to be transported far inland by truck after delivery by ship.

The 503rd jumps onto Corregidor

The Corregidor jump on February 16, 1945, was arguably the most dangerous combat jump of World War II. Casualties were expected to be between 20 and 50 percent. The two small DZs were littered with rubble, twisted rebar, rocks, trees, stumps, wrecked concrete buildings, and bomb and shell craters. Added to that, they were right next to 950ft cliffs which dropped into the sea. The DZs were on the south side of Corregidor's lobe. DZ A was on the parade ground and measured 250 × 325yds. DZ B was on the golf course and was just 185 × 350yds in size. It was expected that there would be 850 Japanese troops on the ground, but that they lacked AA weapons. Machine gun and rifle fire were expected. In reality, there were between 5,000 and 6,000 defenders.

Paratrooper training jumps were generally made from 1,000ft ensuring that there would be time to deploy the reserve parachute. Combat jumps were lower. The Corregidor jump would be from 600ft and a jumper could drift some 1,150ft in the 18-knot wind. Following jumps were from 400ft to improve accuracy. The C-47D transports would fly in trail at 25-second intervals, rather than in "Vs" of three, dropping between six and eight men in each of three passes.

The 503rd PRCT staged on Mindoro 150 miles to the south. After being briefed about the coming operation, the paratroopers were issued six cans of

1/503rd PIR jumpers chute up on Mindoro for the Corregidor jump, February 16, 1945. Note the sacks of yellow Type B-4 inflatable life vests required for overwater flights. Also note the "41" chalked beside the troop door on the C-47D. Each stick (aircraft load) was assigned a chalk number. (Tom Laemlein, Armor Plate Press)

warm beer. They cleaned their weapons and their four grenades, two each of the frag and WP varieties. Their duffel bags were stowed in squad tents. That night they watched a captured film depicting the fall of Corregidor, mistreated American prisoners, and the tearing down of the US flag. The 3/503rd PRCT would be the first to jump followed by the 2nd with the 1st jumping the following day, or being landed amphibiously. They breakfasted on powdered eggs and pancakes at 0530hrs, loaded onto trucks at 0600hrs – each chalk-numbered according to the aircraft the men would jump from – arrived at San José (aka Elmore) and Hill airfields at 0630hrs, chuted up, and boarded 54 C-47s at 0700hrs. Takeoff was 0730hrs. The planes then assembled in formation and were bound for Corregidor 75 minutes away.

Both practice and combat jumps consisted of essentially the same process. Of course, a combat jump was significantly more stressful. Counting parachutes, weapons, ammunition, rations, and equipment each man carried over 80lb. A life vest was donned over their web gear and under their parachute harness. Even with the low attitude, they donned reserves. They had to be aided climbing into the aircraft with the static lines clipped to their reserve's carrying handle. The aircraft's interior was scorching hot and airless. Up to 21 jumpers were carried, seated in plastic seats on both sides of the plane, facing inboard. The jumpmaster sat beside the port side door and the aircraft's loadmaster was nearby. It was common for a larger, experienced paratrooper to bring up the stick's end as the "pusher," ensuring everyone exited.

Troops could smoke. They had to be conscious of their equipment, weapons, and ammunition. There was no moving about the aircraft once strapped into seats. Everyone relieved themselves before chuting up. A long flight with a full bladder was miserable. There was a 10-minute warning. The red light beside the door came on. Those who had removed their helmets strapped them on. The jumpmaster positioned himself to look out of the door to identify the DZ. The 5-minute warning meant smokes out and full attention directed at the jumpmaster. The pilot slowed to 110mph. The jumpmaster stood, hooked up, and using arm and hand signals, gave his jump commands. "Get ready!" They unbuckled their seat belts. "Stand up!" The jumpers stood, helping each other up, and faced the rear. "Hook up!" They uncooked their snaphooks from their reserves and snapped them on the anchor-line cable on the port side and gripped

Troops assemble and assist injured and tangled jumpers on Corregidor. In the background little Caballo Island (Ft Huges) can be seen. (Tom Laemlein, Armor Plate Press)

the static line tightly with their left hands while keeping their balance in the jolting aircraft. "Check static lines." Jumpers ensured their snaphooks were fastened, the retaining pin properly inserted, making sure that the static line was not wrapped around their arm or equipment. They checked the static line of the man in front of them, following it from his shoulder to the backpack. "Check equipment!" They quickly checked their harness snaphooks, equipment and weapon fastenings, and ensured their testicles were not under the legs straps. "Sound off for equipment check!" Each man was assigned a number with the jumpmaster being Number 1. Starting with the last man in the stick they shouted, "Eighteen Okay" and slapped the thigh of the man in front of them. (For Corregidor only six to eight men stood for each pass.) The second man when slapped pointed at the jumpmaster and shouted "Two Okay!" The jumpmaster leaned out the door looking for the landmarks he would have been briefed on and the DZ. When he spotted it he shouted "Stand in the door!" He passed his static line to the loadmaster who kept it from fouling any jumper. Jump commands allowed jumpers to focus totally on what they needed to be doing and not think of the dangers.

The pilot made the final decision to drop and hit the green light. The jumpmaster shouted "Go!" and exited with a leap, pushing hard with his arms to push out from the aircraft. A weak exit could cause tumbling, which could occur anyway owing to the unbalanced weight of equipment and prop-wash. The engines were screaming and prop-wash blasted through the door. There was only a brief sensation of falling which disappeared once the aircraft was out of the field of vision. As the jumper exited he counted "one thousand, two thousand, three thousand." The canopy inflated in about three seconds and opened with a noticeable shock, which was by no means overly uncomfortable. The jumper immediately checked his canopy for tears, looked around to avoid other jumpers, and ensured he was not drifting low over another parachute,

Airdropped ammunition is brought in to an ammunition supply point from the resupply drop zone. Most of the aerial delivery containers and packing materials would be flown out in liaison aircraft and returned to the 408th Airborne Quartermaster Company for re-use. (Tom Laemlein, Armor Plate Press)

1/511th soon moved west into Leyte's central mountains, with the intention of descending the mountains' far side to Ormoc Bay. The Japanese were landing reinforcements there from Luzon. The division CP was soon housed on the Manarawat, a 150ft-high, 200 × 600ft tabletop protected by cliffs on three sides with a gentle slope on the fourth. It was also home to a hospital, supply dumps, a 75mm battery (dropped by parachute – the guns were abandoned when they left the area), and a liaison aircraft strip. It was resupplied by parachute and scores of parachutes were erected for shelter from the sun and rain. A total of 241 personnel were dropped by liaison aircraft in individual jumps to man the base.

The wet rugged jungle-covered 1,400ft hills, cut by gorges and ravines, proved to be very difficult terrain. Navigation was almost impossible and units were located each day by L-5s and their positions were plotted. The trails were slippery, muddy footpaths, crisscrossed by roots. Whatever ammunition and supplies were moved overland were carried by Filipino

Troops enthusiastically read a rare delivery of mail at Manarawat in Leyte's hills, the division forward base. Cargo and troop parachutes were used for shelter. The tent to the left consisted of two buttoned-together ponchos with ration boxes placed over the ridge line to keep out the rain. The 75mm howitzer ammunition packing tube planted in the ground served as a "piss tube." (Tom Laemlein, Armor Plate Press)

The 11th Abn Div's forward base on Leyte at Manarawat was known as "Rayon City" owing to the scores of parachutes erected for shelter from the incessant rain. Other shelters were made from ponchos. The base had the appearance of a hobo camp. (Tom Laemlein, Armor Plate Press)

porters. Communications had to be maintained with temperamental radios, and relay stations had to be established. There was not enough telephone wire and the Japanese were constantly cutting what there was.

The 1st Bn finally made contact with the enemy to the north of Manarawat. The 2nd Bn was sent to reinforce the 1st and the 3rd Bn advanced on a trail to the south of Manarawat to make contact. The wounded had to be carried on poncho litters by six men on a long, grueling 8–10-mile trip to Burauen. In the close terrain engagements tended to be ambushes and short, vicious firefights. There were grenade exchanges and the Japanese used their bipod-mounted light machine guns to good effect, usually to fire down-slope at the Americans. Their riflemen backed up the machine gunners and if they had a large enough force, they tried to outflank the paratroopers. They also employed snipers. The American tripod-mounted M1919A4 machine guns were difficult to set up on the rough ground and fire upslope. They could not be fired as handhelds. BARs were better suited to the conditions.

The first Japanese casualties that the Americans saw were objects of great curiosity. They were left where they fell, the Japanese making no effort to recover them. The passing Americans did not bury them either, unless they were remaining in an area for a time. Sometimes, Filipinos were paid to bury them. The bodies were searched for anything of intelligence value. Souvenir hunters would come next, leaving the bodies with their shirts ripped open and their trousers half down as they were looking for belts of a thousand stitches and flags wrapped around the fallen men's bellies.

 PARATROOPER ON LEYTE, 1944

This 511th PIR grenadier (**1** and **2**) is outfitted in the OD two-piece, the most commonly worn combat uniform in the tropics. It was made of the herringbone fatigue uniform fabric. He also wears the OD Swing cap, which was also made in khaki (**3**). Insignia on the cap varied with possibly a parachutist patch on the left or right (officers) side, airborne tab on the front and sometimes officer rank or jumpwings under it, or there would be simply no insignia. In the 11th Abn Div the Swing cap generally supplemented the paratrooper's cap (garrison cap) worn by other paratroopers. While jungle packs, the top flap compartment of jungle packs, and even gas mask cases were used to carry individual gear, the standard M1936 field bag or "musette bag" continued to be widely used. It could be carried on the back attached to M1936 suspenders or by using a shoulder sling. Paratroopers jumped with a ³⁄₈ or ⁵⁄₈in. diameter, 33ft long parachute rope (**4**). If hung in a tree, the jumper fastened the rope to his harness and climbed down it. It had numerous other field uses. His web gear includes the M1923 cartridge belt with 10 M1 rifle clips, M1942 first aid pouch, M2 jungle first aid kit, M1910 canteen and carrier, an ammunition carrying bag or "general purpose ammo bag" (**5**), M1943 entrenching tool and carrier, and M1 bayonet. An M7 grenade launcher (**6**) is fitted on his rifle on which is an M17 fragmentation grenade. Special grenade launcher cartridges were issued in a strip and stored in a key-opened "spam can" (**7**) which contained 10 M3 cartridges for the rifle, six M6 cartridges for the carbine, and five M7 auxiliary cartridges (which were fitted in the launcher's muzzle to boast the range). Items typically carried in the musette bag and on the paratrooper's person included: an M2 switchblade knife with a 3¹⁄₈in. blade (**8**), leather riding gloves (**9**), mosquito repellent (**10**), a D-ration bar (**11**), foot powder (**12**), halazone water purification tablets (**13**), an M-210 message book (**14**), a pocket compass (**15**), a match container (**16**), rifle oil (**17**), rifle bore cleaner (**18**), and an M1926 spoon (**19**).

8

6

3

5

7

9

18

17

10

4

1

2

16

13

19

Message Book M-210
Signal Corps U.S. Army

14

U.S. ARMY FIELD RATION D

11

HALAZONE

FOOT
POWDER

12

15

The 11th Abn Div's support troops in the division rear on Leyte assisted with rear area security. Japanese infiltrators were a continuous problem. Here, M1 rifle and M1A1 carbine-armed service troops hunt for Japanese snipers. (Tom Laemlein, Armor Plate Press)

Some troops wore the two-piece fatigues and others the one-piece coveralls. While the one-piece was warmer, took longer to dry, and required web gear to be removed and the suit to be stripped down to the legs to relieve oneself, it had one advantage. When crawling through mud and dead leaves it prevented the shirt from coming out of the trousers and goop working its way in. The soles started coming off constantly wet jump boots owing to hard walking. Few received airdropped replacements and had to tape or tie the soles on. Men carried six or seven pairs of socks, but they were impossible to dry even when tied on the outside of their packs. The rain, dripping trees, and overcast skies prevented drying.

Mosquitoes swarmed. Troops had mosquito head nets, but these restricted vision and hearing, especially at night when mosquitoes were at their worst. Instead, they doused themselves with insect repellent, which did nothing to help their body odor, which was made worse by sweat, grime, and mud. As well as being used to dig foxholes, entrenching tools were used for digging latrines. While on the move, the soldier would step off to the trailside, dig a cat hole, do his business, and trot to catch up with his squad. In a foxhole he would move quietly to the rear and dig a cat hole. Soldiers failing to dig a cat hole were chastised, as almost all had dysentery. It was unpleasant enough as it was. Toilet paper proved to be a valuable commodity with too little provided in K-rations.

Foxholes were dug after dark, when the Japanese could not see where a unit was digging in and how it was deployed. The overcast nights were pitch black. Listening was more important than night vision. The troops remained completely quiet. They would have eaten before dark and usually before moving into their night positions. Two- and three-man foxholes were dug up to 4ft deep and between five and 15yds apart, depending on vegetation density. Digging was not too difficult once the rain-soaked first foot was worked through and if there were not too many difficult roots. One man in each position was on guard for two hours with time kept by an issue luminous dial watch passed from man to man. It was a common practice for a weary soldier to watch and listen for a spell, set the watch ahead, and wake his buddy. Who in turn would set the watch ahead and so on for a lot of short "two-hour" watches.

A couple of weeks into the operation, the paratroopers were adapting to the realities of combat. They accepted that death came suddenly and indiscriminately. Close calls were the norm. It made no difference if a man had been a star soldier in training or a dud. They also soon realized the Japanese were not 10ft tall nor were they necessarily good jungle fighters. Certainly, they were no better than the paratroopers themselves. It was apparent that the Americans were better trained, armed, equipped, and led. Pfc Deane E. Marks, a member of the 2/511th's Light Machine Gun Platoon, commented on the enemy:

> You couldn't see 5ft in front of you and your imagination would run rampant. You would visualize a Nip right out in front of you, getting ready to lob a grenade at you. There were Japanese out there and one consolation was they were just as wet, muddy and cold as we were. I always felt they were "scared" of us. We were certainly not afraid of them, but felt eager to search them out and do them in. Sitting in your foxhole at night and waiting to see if they would try to slip through was something else. You just were full of anxieties and had the feeling that a particular Nip was out to get you.

In early December they reached Mahonag, an oval clearing on the mountains' west slope known as the "Potato Patch" – they dug up native potatoes in the clearing. This was established as a base, resupplied by parachute, and signaled a pause in operations. The paratroopers conducted patrols on the trails leading to Ormoc Bay. As buddies were lost, Japanese-hunting patrols were dispatched to clear the area of the rear guard and snipers. This was done just as much for revenge as for security.

The wounded were collected at Mahonag and sheltered under cargo parachutes on litters that had been airdropped. There were not enough blankets and ponchos. The seriously wounded could not be evacuated until enough Filipinos were collected to carry them to Manarawat where they could be evacuated by liaison aircraft. Medical personnel had arrived to care for them, but some didn't make it. Severely damaged limbs had to be

511th PIR paratroopers examine a trophy Japanese 7.7mm Type 99 (1939) Nambu light machine gun. Note that the second soldier from the right wears jumpwings, which were seldom seen in the field. (Tom Laemlein, Armor Plate Press)

A wounded paratrooper is carried to the regimental aid station on Leyte. The man to the left is armed with an M1 carbine, the sling of which has been replaced with a white .30-cal machine gun belt in which smaller .30 Carbine cartridges have been loaded. 75mm howitzer rounds are beneath the canvas tarp in the lower left. (Tom Laemlein, Armor Plate Press)

amputated where, in other circumstances, they could have been saved. There wasn't enough plasma or morphine. In the meantime the "limpers," walking wounded capable of making their way to Manarawat, were dispatched in small groups, escorted and assisted by scratch squads. It was a grueling trip over the slippery up-and-down trails. The rain continued and the trails oozed muck. Everyone was perpetually wet.

The paratroopers had managed to cut the Japanese supply line for their attempted counterattack across the island toward Burauen. As the paratroopers approached the bay they received artillery fire for the first time. Several salvos caught the lead elements of 2/511th as they approached the Japanese strongpoint on Rock Hill. The shattering explosions were a new shock cutting down dozens of men, with some suffering severed limbs. The attack was called off leaving some dozen dead and almost 40 wounded. It required a great deal of manpower, using poncho litters, to get the dead and wounded back to Mahonag. The American dead were buried inside the perimeter in marked graves, to be recovered later.

The 77th Inf Div was attacking from the north and pushing more Japanese down the bay's shore towards the 511th. The 511th's drastically reduced strength forced them to pull back to Mahonag. There was no depth to the defensive position, just a tight perimeter of foxholes. As they were close to the bay, fog moved in making aerial resupply impossible. Within two days they ran out of K-rations. The bodies of the Japanese dead were searched for chow and it was found the Japanese were taking Ks from American dead. The men talked and dreamt of food. Since there were streams in the area they shaved daily and bathed by simply wading into the water. Regardless of the rain, insects were abundant. However, snakes were never seen. The Japanese made persistent attacks and suffered for it. Most American casualties were lost to snipers. After several days, the fog dissipated and C-47s and L-5s were able to drop ammunition, rations, and medical supplies. Some heavy cases broke loose and one man was killed as others dodged falling ammunition crates. Some men

The 221st Airborne Medical Company's operating room on Leyte. Conditions were extremely crude and unsanitary. (Tom Laemlein, Armor Plate Press)

ate until they puked being unable to tolerate K-rations. The Japanese managed to recover some misdropped supplies, including 81mm mortar ammunition – US and Japanese 81mm ammunition was interchangeable.

With the resupply drops, the Japanese backed off and 2/511th again pushed toward 3/511th nearer to the bay. They had to fight their way through Japanese positions and found the 3/511th to be in bad shape. The Japanese had only a little rice, their split-toe shoes were rotting and their uniforms were in rags. They had dug deep bunkers for protection from artillery and mortars, but had suffered many casualties from indirect fire.

The 511th was finally relieved by the 187th Glider Inf and followed the glidermen to the bay. It took 250 men to carry their wounded to the field hospital set up near the beach. A bivouac was established down the beach and there they were issued with new fatigues and jungle hammocks. The latter had an integral rain-cover and mosquito netting on the sides and ends. The men

11th Abn Div troops on Leyte unload canned turkey for their 1944 Christmas dinner from a Piper L-4 Grasshopper. The division's 35 L-4 and L-5 liaison aircraft were instrumental in keeping frontline units supplied by airdrop. (Tom Laemlein, Armor Plate Press)

felt like royalty sleeping high and dry for once. They bathed in the ocean and were clean for the first time in a month. On Christmas Day they had turkey with all the trimmings and ice cream. They all left buddies in the jungle. Pfc Deane E. Marks summed it up:

> There always was that feeling of, "Glad it wasn't me." We all felt bad, for a short time, when a buddy was killed, but deep inside, you were thankful to God that the shrapnel or bullet didn't take you. I never saw anyone who was willing to trade places with a corpse. We were so tired and burned out that all we wanted was to be left alone.

AFTERMATH OF BATTLE

The 511th PIR fought a relatively short, but difficult, 37-day campaign on Leyte after sea delivery. It went on to central Luzon where it was delivered by parachute to fight in jungles, hills, and urban areas for 90 days. It then reversed direction and cleared southern Luzon for another 69 days. A final operation saw 1st Bn, 511th, operate in northern Luzon on a simple 11-day operation. The 503rd PIR experienced 168 days of combat and the 511th PIR 196 days plus 11 additional days for its 1st Bn.

The 511th PIR sustained a total of 211 killed, 10 missing, and 960 wounded during the Leyte and Luzon campaigns. The 503rd suffered 339 dead and missing.

The Currahee Military Museum is located in the old railroad station in Toccoa, GA. A memorial to the parachute regiments raised at Camp Toccoa was established in 1990 at the old camp entrance on Old Highway 123. The camp itself was closed in 1946 and only one original building remains on factory grounds. Perhaps the most enduring memorial to the paratroopers will never disappear – Currahee Mountain dominates the horizon 2 miles to the southeast.

The 11th Abn Div would remain in Japan on occupation duty at Yokohama. Later, it was moved north for duty on Honshu and Hokkaido

1/511th PIR troops assemble on Appari Airfield after jumping in at Camalaniugan, Luzon on February 23, 1945. The radio jeep and trailer were delivered by CG-4A gliders, two of the six used can be seen in the background. Several Filipino guerrillas, who were waiting on the drop zone after securing the area before the drop, can be seen. (Tom Laemlein, Armor Plate Press)

islands. In May 1949 the division returned to the States and was stationed at Ft Campbell, KY, as a training division until the outbreak of the Korean War when it was converted to a combat division. Its 187th Abn Inf Regt[7] was deployed to Korea in September 1950, being brought up to strength by men from the 511th. In 1956 the 11th Abn Div relocated to Augsburg, West Germany. It remained there until July 1, 1958, when it was inactivated and its assets used to organize the 24th Inf Div, which maintained an airborne capability. With the inactivation of the 11th, the 511th Abn Inf Regt was also inactivated. In February 1963 the 11th Air Assault Div (TEST) was reactivated with 1/511th Inf as a non-airborne battalion. The experimental division was inactivated in July 1965 when its assets were absorbed into the 1st Cavalry Div (Airmobile) and the 511th has not since been reactivated, with one exception. In 1997 A/511th PIR was activated as a test unit for the Enhanced Fiber Optic Guided Missile system and later inactivated.

SELECT BIBLIOGRAPHY

Devlin, Gerard M., *Back to Corregidor: America Retakes the Rock*. St Martins Press, New York (1992)

Flanagan, Edward M. Jr., *Corregidor: The Rock Force Assault*, Presidio, Novato, CA (1988)

Flanagan, Edward M. Jr., *The Angels: A History of the 11th Airborne Division 1943–46*, Infantry Journal Press, Washington, DC (1948)

FM 31-30, *Tactics and Techniques of Air-Borne Troops*, (May 1942)

Gabel, Kurt, *The Making of a Paratrooper: Airborne Training and Combat in World War II*, University Press of Kansas, Lawrence (1990)

Huston, James A., *Out of the Blue: U.S. Army Airborne Operations in World War II*, Purdue University Press, West Lafayette, IN (1973)

ABOVE LEFT
An 11th Abn Div jeep patrol on Luzon. An airborne division had only 283 ¼-ton jeeps, 20 ¾-ton trucks, and 82 2½-ton trucks. A standard infantry division had over 1,300 trucks of all types. (Tom Laemlein, Armor Plate Press)

ABOVE
A Piper L-4 Grasshopper liaison airplane is loaded aboard a Douglas C-54 Skymaster transport. The big four-engine transports, assembled from all over the world, airlifted the 11th Abn Div from Okinawa to Japan in a week. (Tom Laemlein, Armor Plate Press)

7 In 1947–48 the parachute and glider infantry regiments were all given parachute and glider capabilities and redesignated as "airborne infantry." Glider training ceased in 1949 and the capability was eliminated in 1953.

INDEX